CONSTELLATIONS

Like the future itself, the imaginative possibilities of science fiction are limitless. And the very development of cinema is inextricably linked to the genre, which, from the earliest depictions of space travel and the robots of silent cinema to the immersive 3D wonders of contemporary blockbusters, has continually pushed at the boundaries. **Constellations** provides a unique opportunity for writers to share their passion for science fiction cinema in a book-length format, each title devoted to a significant film from the genre. Writers place their chosen film in a variety of contexts – generic, institutional, social, historical – enabling **Constellations** to map the terrain of science fiction cinema from the past to the present... and the future.

'This stunning, sharp series of books fills a real need for authoritative, compact studies of key science fiction films. Written in a direct and accessible style by some of the top critics in the field, brilliantly designed, lavishly illustrated and set in a very modern typeface that really shows off the text to best advantage, the volumes in the **Constellations** series promise to set the standard for SF film studies in the 21st century.'
Wheeler Winston Dixon, Ryan Professor of Film Studies, University of Nebraska

 Constellations

Constelbooks

Also available in this series

12 Monkeys Susanne Kord

Blade Runner Sean Redmond

Brainstorm Joseph Maddrey

Children of Men Dan Dinello

Close Encounters of the Third Kind Jon Towlson

The Damned Nick Riddle

Dune Christian McCrea

Ex Machina Joshua Grimm

Inception David Carter

Jurassic Park Paul Bullock

Lost Brigid Cherry

Mad Max Martyn Conterio

RoboCop Omar Ahmed

Rollerball Andrew Nette

Stalker Jon Hoel

The Stepford Wives Samantha Lindop

Forthcoming

Aliens Cristina Massaccesi

Minority Report D. Harlan Wilson

Moon Brian J Robb

Mr Freedom Tyler Sage

CONSTELLATIONS

The OA

David Sweeney

Acknowledgements

Many, many thanks to the following for support and/or guidance during the writing of this book:

LJ, VZ and all the Ducks; Alexandra Bland; Prof. Gordon J. Hush; Dr Andrew D. Crighton; Steven Duffy; Martin Sweeney; C.J. Mitchell; and my friends and colleagues in the Department of Design History and Theory at The Glasgow School of Art.

Major thanks too to John Atkinson at Auteur/LUP for commissioning the book in the first place and for infinite patience with me afterwards.

And, of course, my deepest gratitude to Brit Marling and Zal Batmanglij for creating the rich and endlessly rewarding world(s) of *The OA*. Looking forward to your next movement...

First published in 2022 by
Auteur, an imprint of
Liverpool University Press,
4 Cambridge Street,
Liverpool L69 7ZU
www.liverpooluniversitypress.co.uk/imprints/Auteur/
Copyright © Auteur 2022

Series design: Nikki Hamlett at Cassels Design
Set by Cassels Design, Luton, UK.

All rights reserved. No part of this publication may be reproduced in any material form (including photocopying or storing in any medium by electronic means and whether or not transiently or incidentally to some other use of this publication) without the permission of the copyright owner.

Figures from *The OA* © Anonymous Content / Plan B / Netflix

British Library Cataloguing-in-Publication Data
A catalogue record for this book is available from the British Library

ISBN paperback: 978-1-80085-943-2
ISBN hardback: 978-1-80085-942-5
ISBN PDF: 978-1-80085-856-5

Contents

Introduction 7

Synopsis 11

Chapter 1: *The OA* as a Brit Marling and Zal Batmanglij Collaboration 15

Chapter 2: *The OA* as a Streaming Serialised Drama 25

Chapter 3: *The OA* and Genre 45

Chapter 4: *The OA* and the Real World 73

Chapter 5: Influences and Comparable Texts 87

Conclusion 101

Notes 105

Works Cited 106

Introduction

The OA (2016–19) was a streaming television series released as part of Netflix's 'Originals' line of programming, produced by and made available exclusively on the platform. It comprised two seasons, or 'parts' as the programme-makers preferred to name them, each consisting of eight episodes identified onscreen as 'chapters'. The first season originally aired in December 2016, the second in March 2019. In both cases, the entire season was uploaded – or 'dumped' – onto the Netflix platform at once. The series was created, and executive produced, by Brit Marling and Zal Batmanglij. Marling starred in the lead role as Prairie Johnson, appearing in every episode but one (the sixth episode of season two), and is credited with co-writing ten of the sixteen episodes, seven of them with Batmanglij (although the writing-by-committee convention of American television production, and their status as series creators and executive producers, means that the two were undoubtedly involved in the scripting of every episode). Batmanglij directed every episode of season one and all but three episodes of season two. The series was cancelled by Netflix after the second season, in August 2019.

According to the review-aggregation website Rotten Tomatoes, as of the time of writing, the first season of *The OA* has a 77% approval rating from critics and a 78% audience approval rating; the ratings for season two are 92% from critics and 89% from the audience. Nevertheless, *The OA* has received negative criticism in high profile publications such as *The Guardian* and *Variety*. For Jack Seale (2019) in the former, the series is, ultimately, 'rubbish, but handsomely mounted rubbish' while *Variety*'s Sonia Saraiya dismissed it as 'self-indulgent, self-serious psychodrama' (2016). There is a suggestion here, and elsewhere, that *The OA* is somehow lacking in authenticity, particularly when compared to similar series such as *Twin Peaks* (1990-91; 2017) or *Sense8* (2015-18), another Netflix Originals series which was also cancelled after two seasons. Marling and Batmanglij are often accused of having crowded the series with under-developed ideas, perhaps, as another critic, Sean Hutchinson of *Inverse* magazine argues (2017), as a result of the opportunities provided to them by Netflix's financial largesse and indulgence of artistic freedom, which I address in Chapter 2. As I will demonstrate through a close reading of the series, however, there is a strong thematic and diegetic consistency both within and between each season which strongly suggests that what may appear to be an under-developed idea can instead be seen as an element of foreshadowing or world-building which would have been resolved or consolidated if the series had not been cancelled and the creators had been able to deliver on their planned five-season vision (Travers, 2018). As such, *The OA* provides a novel viewing experience which requires a certain investment and patience from its audience as its complex narrative unfolds over seasons as well as between episodes – and, given the establishment of the existence of the multiverse in the second season, also across dimensions.

Unique though I argue *The OA* may be, I also, in Chapters 3 and 5 identify other works of fiction to which it may be usefully compared, including those which may have influenced it. I also address, in Chapter 4, real-life events which may have served as sources of inspiration for Marling and Batmanglij. As an example of both a work of fiction and of a real-life event I pay particular attention, in Chapter 4, to *The Institute*, Spencer McCall's 2013 film about the Augmented Reality/Live Action Role Play Game *The Jejune Institute*, created by Jeff Hull, which, like the game itself, blurs the boundaries between documentary and drama. Although neither Marling nor Batmanglij have, to my knowledge, ever publicly mentioned either McCall's film or Hull's game, *The OA*'s indebtedness to it is, as I will demonstrate, undeniable. To be clear, I do not suggest that Marling and Batmanglij are in any way guilty of plagiarism. Rather, I discuss the game and the film in terms of the two's uses of source material, including the actual world events (Hull's game really did unfold, in San Francisco and, to a lesser extent, Oakland between 2008 and 2011) discussed in Chapter 4 which they fictionalise in a similar way to the manner in which Prairie appears to in *The OA*'s first season. A similar fictionalising approach appears to be taken by the character Maggie, also played by Marling, in her first collaborative project with Batmanglij, the independent psychological thriller *Sound of My Voice* (2011) which may also be a time travel narrative, depending on the viewer's interpretation (as I discuss in Chapter 1), along with their second co-production, the studio-funded feature film *The East* (2013). In this chapter I also address *Another Earth* (2011), Marling's collaboration with another director, Mike Cahill, which contains thematic elements later developed in *The OA*. The other texts to which I compare

The OA, in Chapters 3 and, particularly, 5 are presented in order to give historical and generic context for the series.

The elements of world-building and foreshadowing mentioned above were, of course, frustrated by the cancellation of the series, which looks unlikely to continue either on another network or in another medium; furthermore, the ending of the second season, as well as being the expected cliff-hanger, also calls into question the ontological status of everything that has gone before, leaving the committed viewer also in a state of frustration. It also, however, inspires speculation: Marling (2019) has encouraged fans of the series to continue 'authoring' the story, which some have done in the form of fan fiction – including film-making as well as writing – as I discuss in my Conclusion where I also provide my own speculation as to how the series may have developed after the second season. The 'authoring' Marling writes of refers too to the protest staged by fans against the series' cancellation, represented on line by the hashtag SaveTheOA, and the use by fans of the choreographed movements performed by the group Prairie forms as a type of participatory community activity which I also discuss in the Conclusion. I also address the sale, online, of merchandise associated with the protest but unauthorised by Netflix as well as the way in which fans involved in #SaveTheOA have drawn upon the themes, concerns, imagery and symbolism of the series in their response to the quarantine measures and restrictions on physical social interaction imposed internationally following the outbreak of the coronavirus pandemic of 2020.

Synopsis

Part I

After having disappeared seven years earlier at the age of 21, a young blind woman, Prairie Johnson, returns to the home of her adoptive parents, Nancy and Abel, in the Michigan suburb of Crestview. Miraculously, Prairie's sight has been restored. Although she will not explain her absence to her parents or to the authorities, Prairie gathers a group of four teenage boys from the local high school and one of their teachers in an abandoned house in the suburb and, over the course of the season, narrates the story of her time away to them. According to Prairie, she had been held captive in an underground dungeon with four others by a scientist named Hap who is convinced that people who have suffered Near Death Experiences (NDEs) – as Prairie and her fellow captives all have – have glimpsed the afterlife. Hap is determined to share their vision. He experiments on his prisoners by 'killing' them under laboratory conditions for fixed periods of time before reviving them and extrapolating data from their experiences. Hap eventually comes to realise that NDEs in fact provide a glimpse of other dimensions within a multiverse, rather than of an afterlife; dimensions to which he is also determined to travel. During one NDE, Prairie is informed of her true status as the Original Angel: the OA of the series' title. Prairie and the other captives have acquired knowledge during their NDEs of four of five movements which, if performed together as a group, will allow inter-dimensional travel. Prairie plans for them to use these movements to escape from Hap. Hap learns of Prairie's plans and intends to use the movements for his own purposes. Hap is discovered by a local police officer; Hap convinces the policeman that Prairie is capable of curing his terminally ill wife. Prairie does so and the woman, who had experienced an NDE of her own, provides her, and Hap, with the final movement required for inter-dimensional travel. Hap then kills her and her husband, and prepares his escape to another dimension. After releasing Prairie, he assembles his prisoners and forces them to perform the movements.

Back in the present, French, one of Prairie's group who has had doubts about her story all along, even while the others become increasingly convinced of her narrative and devoted to her, breaks into her family home and discovers a box of books which seem to have provided the source material for Prairie's tale. Disillusioned, he shares this revelation with the group, which breaks up. They resume their lives separately at school; as they are doing so, a shooter enters the campus and opens fire. The scene cuts to Prairie running towards the school. Back at the school, the shooter has entered the cafeteria; the group use the movements to distract him momentarily, which allows a kitchen worker to overpower the shooter whose weapon goes off in the struggle. As it does so, Prairie, who had also been performing the movements off-camera outside the cafeteria, is wounded in the chest by a stray bullet. The episode, and season, closes with one of the group, Steven, running after the ambulance which has taken Prairie away after he realises that the group's movements have not only distracted the shooter but also opened a portal between dimensions allowing Prairie's consciousness to travel to the dimension where her fellow captives have gone. The episode ends with a close up of a seemingly confused Prairie against a white background uncertainly speaking the name of the prisoner, Homer, with whom she had fallen in love during their shared captivity.

Part 2

The second season takes place largely in the parallel dimension into which Prairie has jumped following her apparent death at the end of the first season. There she possesses the body of her counterpart, Nina Azarova, a wealthy businesswoman with ties to the Russian mafia. Hap and his captives have also jumped to this dimension and entered their counterparts' bodies there. Hap has become Dr Percy, head of a psychiatric facility in San Francisco in which his captives are inmates with the exception of Homer, who is Dr Roberts, a psychiatrist on Percy's staff who cannot remember his previous identity. A new character, private investigator Karim Washington, is employed to investigate the disappearance of this dimension's counterpart to one of the members of Prairie's group, Buck. His investigations lead him to Prairie who, as Nina, is also an inmate in Hap's facility, Hap having recognized Prairie in Nina's body. Karim helps Prairie escape and together they enter a mysterious house in the city's Nob Hill district which is later revealed to be an interdimensional portal.

Meanwhile, back in the dimension of the first season the members of the group, who are mourning Prairie, are contacted by the consciousness of one of the captives, Rachel, who instructs them on how to find Prairie. In the parallel dimension, Prairie confronts Hap who reveals he has built a map of the multiverse using human subjects, including the counterparts of Prairie's group. Hap attempts to kill Prairie but she becomes imbued with a supernatural power and begins to ascend into the sky in front of him. However, her ascension is interrupted and she jumps to yet another dimension, followed by Hap and witnessed by Karim from the attic of the Nob Hill house, falling to the floor of a soundstage on which a TV series which appears to be a version of *The OA* is being filmed. Stunned by this sight, Karim notices Buck and calls on him by the name Michelle. Buck goes to him causing the inter-dimensional portal to collapse. Prairie has entered the body of her counterpart who in this new dimension is an actor called Brit, who has been severely injured on-set. Hap arrives in his counterpart, a version of the actor Jason Isaacs who plays Hap. He informs medical personnel arriving on the scene that he is Brit's husband. Brit is taken away in an ambulance accompanied by Hap who has sublimated Isaacs's consciousness to his own. Suddenly the ambulance door opens and Steven enters, greeting Hap by name.

Chapter I: *The OA* as a Brit Marling and Zal Batmanglij Collaboration

Figure 1: Prairie Johnson – Traveller of the Multiverse.

In this section, I briefly place *The OA* in the context of Marling and Batmanglij's previous collaborations, the feature films *Sound of My Voice* and *The East*, identifying consistent narrative themes, diegetic techniques and production practices. I also address *Another Earth*, Marling's collaboration with another director, Mike Cahill, which contains thematic elements later developed in *The OA*.

Sound of My Voice

The OA bears strong similarities to Marling and Batmanglij's first feature-length collaboration *Sound of My Voice*, released in 2011 (after the 2007 short *The Recordist*, written and directed by Batmanglij and starring Marling). Like *The OA*, the film focuses on a small group of marginalised individuals organised around a charismatic leader played by Marling. In *The OA* this leader is Prairie; in *Sound of My Voice* it is Maggie, a self-proclaimed time traveller from the year 2054 who has come to the Los Angeles of 2014 to warn of an imminent civil war which will destroy

American society. Like the group in *The OA* who meet in an abandoned house to hear Prairie's life story, Maggie's followers also gather in a suburban home to listen to her accounts of what is to come. Maggie is always seen dressed entirely in white and attached to an oxygen tank on which she claims to be reliant because she is allergic to the toxins of the industrialised twenty-first century. Maggie's followers grow organic fruit and vegetables in an attempt to avoid polluting their bodies with the 'poison' of the modern world; according to Maggie the 'bullshit' world-view of potential new followers is similarly toxic. All her followers strive to achieve a similar state of physical purity and mental clarity as their leader. In the first episode of *The OA*, Prairie, posing as Steve's mother in an attempt to prevent him from being expelled from school, defends his unruly behaviour by remarking 'it's not really a measure of mental health to be well-adjusted in a society that's very sick', echoing Maggie's views of modernity.

In their all-white uniform and with the religious awe with which they regard Maggie, her followers resemble a cult and the group is considered to be so by the two aspiring documentary film-makers, Peter (Christopher Denham) and Lorna (Nicole Vicius), who infiltrate it in an attempt to expose Maggie as a fraud. As the sociologist Peter L. Berger has observed (1969), the existence of cults is itself a symptom of secularisation, a consequence of what another, earlier, sociologist, Max Weber, writing in the early twentieth century, identified as the 'disenchantment' of the Western world following the Enlightenment and the resulting paradigm shift from a religious and magical understanding of the world to one rooted in science and rationalism (2003). Maggie's followers display a kind of spiritual hunger and longing for meaning in their lives; Prairie's appear to be similarly troubled, even the seemingly popular and flourishing Alfonso 'French' Sosa (Brandon Perea) whose academic and athletic success at school belies a dysfunctional home life. The other members are Steve (Patrick Gibson), a rather macho individual, who deals drugs in the neighbourhood and is also something of a school bully, with ambitions to become a fitness trainer to the rich and famous as well as an online celebrity in his own right; Jesse (Brendan Meyer) an orphan and 'stoner' who is Steve's partner in his drug business as well as his filming the 'stunts' Steve performs for his YouTube channel; Buck (Ian Alexander), a transgender boy who seems drawn to Prairie from the outset and is perhaps the most loyal to her; and Betty Broderick-Allen (Phyllis Smith), known as BBA, a teacher at the boys' high school who is grieving the recent loss of her brother and who also struggles with issues pertaining to over-eating. Marling has spoken, in a 2016 interview with Debra Birnbaum for *Variety* magazine's website, of recognising a sense of 'dislocation' amongst teenage boys at the mid-Western high schools she and Batmanglij visited as research for *The OA*, recalling Weber's contemporary and colleague, Emile Durkheim's concept of anomie or 'normlessness': a sense of a cultural break from tradition (2013). For Marling, this dislocation in teenage boys is the result of a lack of empowerment, and the absence of an equivalent for them of the empowering narrative of feminism. Joining Prairie's group re-connects them with, as Marling puts it, 'something wild', by which she seems to mean their masculinity, which has been compromised, as she wrote elsewhere, by the 'increasingly toxic obligations of American manhood' (2020) and with a sense of purpose comparable to the empowering feeling of purposefulness Maggie instils her group. Access to Maggie is firmly controlled by an inner circle of attendants who use an elaborate handshake to greet each other and initiate new recruits, which anticipates the elaborate dance moves required, according to Prairie, to travel between dimensions in *The OA*, emphasising her cult's secretive and esoteric nature just as the movements unite Prairie's group in shared esoteric knowledge.

Weber observed that the authority of charismatic leaders is usually associated with religion, the word 'charisma' being derived from the Ancient Greek term for divinely conferred grace: χάρισμα. However, Weber also applied the term in a secular context, noting that charismatic leaders are perceived as possessing a 'certain quality of an individual personality, by virtue of which [they are] set apart from ordinary men and treated as endowed with supernatural, superhuman, or at least specifically exceptional powers or qualities' (2003: 358). Some of Prairie's followers initially doubt her claims – particularly the aggressive Steve, who is failing at school, but also the practical minded, high-achieving French – but even they are captivated by her charisma as a storyteller, their doubts over the fantastic elements of her story notwithstanding. The provable facts of Prairie's tale – that she did disappear seven years earlier and that she has recovered her sight – provide her a degree of both exceptionalism and credibility as well as an alluring air of Otherness. Maggie's story in *Sound of My Voice* is also based around a fantastic claim, that of time travel, which is represented in the film as having been undertaken by mystical rather than technological means in as much as it is explained at all. Maggie does not make any further claims regarding the supernatural, at least not on-screen, and, in a private meeting with Peter, smokes tobacco and drinks alcohol, telling him she is not 'a saint', which also suggests to the viewer that Maggie's use of the oxygen tank may be merely be part of her ruse. While neither Maggie nor Prairie, for the most part, demonstrate any 'supernatural' or 'superhuman' powers to their followers, although they do make claims for them, their very presence has an enchanting effect on the audience for their narratives, which is a power in and of itself: that of charisma. This is communicated, in both film and series, by Marling's compelling performances and Batmanglij's treatment of her face. Highly photogenic, Marling's cover model[1] features can at times make her appear impassive and aloof, particularly when she is not speaking, but even then there is usually a sense, communicated by her expressive eyes, that such affective blankness masks hidden pain or turmoil.

The communicative power of Marling's features is central to a key scene from *Sound of My Voice* in which one of Maggie's followers asks her to sing a song from the future. Laughing nervously, yet endearingly, Maggie reluctantly obliges with a shaky, unaccompanied rendition of 'Dreams', a 1993 hit single by Irish alternative rock group The Cranberries, delivered with a palpable air of vulnerability, particularly in the lyric 'You have my heart so don't hurt me' which comes across as a direct appeal by Maggie to the cult. As the song unfolds, Batmanglij cuts between Maggie, in her awkwardness, and the serene state of her followers who listen with eyes closed, except for Peter, his partner Lorna, and an elderly woman, Joanne (Kandice Stroh, who co-starred in Batmanglij's *The Recordist* with Marling), later revealed to be one of Maggie's most loyal acolytes, who gazes directly at Maggie as she joins in the song's refrain which is familiar to her, as it is to the rest of the cult because of its provenance as a '90s hit single. The woman's belief in Maggie is not tested by her familiarity with the song, however, nor does the rest of the group appear to be troubled afterwards – including Peter, who seems to fall for Maggie both ideologically and emotionally at this point – with the exception of Lorna, who displays a mixture of astonishment and disgust at Maggie's audacity in using such a well-known piece of music as evidence of her futuristic origins, and a male follower (Alvin Lam) who, while insisting that he 'means no disrespect', points out the origin of the song to Maggie. Maggie's response, delivered after her face assumes an offended expression suggestive too of a barely controlled anger, is to claim ignorance because she 'wasn't alive in the '90s' and to explain that, in her time, when recorded music is scarce, the song is associated with a folk singer named Benetton. If she is lying about being a time traveller, Maggie's choice of such a recognisable song as 'Dreams' is nevertheless a highly effective tactic to emphasise her Otherness to her followers, as is her nervous, acapella delivery of it which contrasts sharply with the oratorical confidence displayed in her earlier addresses to the group. Both the song choice and her delivery, including her nervousness before singing and evident relief immediately afterwards, serve to affirm her charismatic authority precisely because they make her vulnerable, creating empathy in her followers, and perhaps in the viewer too.

The suggestion that a fantastical, but allegedly true, story may have been constructed from mundane sources is recalled in the final episode of season one of *The OA* when French discovers of a box of books hidden in Prairie's bedroom after his doubts have driven him to break into her home. The books include the classical text *The Iliad* by Homer, also the name of one of Prairie's fellow prisoners with whom she claims to have fallen in love, and Pulitzer prize winner David E. Hoffman's *The Oligarchs: Wealth and Power in the New Russia*, both of which exist in the actual world of the viewer. The box also contains two invented texts: *An Encyclopaedia of Near Death Experiences* and *The Book of Angels* by fictional authors Dr Kevin Chang and Audrey Ebbs respectively (whose names are also those of the first assistant accountant [Chang] and an associate producer [Ebbs] on *The OA*, according to IMDb), which have the appearance of mass market publications. Prairie appears to have drawn on all four for the story – of being the daughter of an assassinated Russian oligarch who has had an NDE, which is how she learned about angels, why she has been abducted by Hap and how she met Homer – with which she enthralled the group. French's discovery of these books discomfits him, confirming his earlier doubts about her but also reviving the sense of 'dislocation' or *anomie* he experienced prior to entering into Prairie's orbit. Buck's faith in Prairie is unshaken after French shows the group the books, however, recalling Peter's seemingly full conversion to belief in Maggie at the end of *Sound of My Voice*, even as he admits he doesn't know who she really is. Buck's faith is demonstrated in his decision to retain *The Book of Angels* as a souvenir of his time with Prairie and the others, and also as a kind of talisman for his life henceforth. Being with Prairie has given Buck a sense of purpose just as Peter finds with Maggie in *Sound of My Voice*. For Weber (2003), purposelessness was a symptom of the secularisation of the modern world resulting from its disenchantment; the mysticism of Prairie's story, and of her quest to liberate her fellow prisoners from Hap's clutches, offers both a purpose to her followers and a re-enchantment of their lives just as Maggie's own mystical arrival in 2014 does for the cult that forms around her.

Marling herself discusses *The OA* with reference to *Sound of My Voice* in her interview with Birnbaum, remarking that the 'delicious thing' about the film's ambiguity over whether or not Maggie really is a time-traveller, which is not resolved in its climax, is the tendency for audiences to 'really take sides'. This brings to mind the response to Russian novelist Vladimir Nabokov's English language novel *Pale Fire* (1962) by readers who align themselves with either the character John Shade or that of Charles Kinbote depending on which one they believe is the true narrator of the book, taking the side of either 'Shadean' or 'Kinbotean' in debates surrounding the text. The literary theorist Brian McHale has described *Pale Fire* as a novel of 'absolute epistemological uncertainty' (1987: 18) because there is no definitive proof either way as to the identity of the true narrator, Kinbote or Shade (or even another figure, Professor Botkin, for whom Kinbote is an alter ego). This description could equally apply to *Sound of My Voice* and to the first season of *The OA*, both of which end on an ambiguous note. Nabokov is evoked too in Prairie's backstory: like her, Nabokov was both a member of a wealthy and powerful Russian family and, subsequently, an exile from the country, in his case following the October Revolution of 1917, which would see him, again like Prairie, ultimately settle in the US. The Russian dolls which appear in both seasons also bring to mind the nested narration of *Pale Fire* (I discuss the dolls further in Chapters 2 and 3).

A final point of comparison lies in the mystery surrounding the character Carol Briggs (Davenia McFadden), who claims to be a Justice Department agent in pursuit of Maggie but seems to be rather more than that – I have previously suggested she too may be a time traveller (2015). In this she anticipates *The OA*'s Elias Rahim (Riz Ahmed), Prairie's FBI counsellor in season one who reveals himself, in the second season (episode six), to be not only aware of Prairie angelic status but to have been tasked by an unnamed entity with helping her. Rahim's role in the narrative would, presumably, have been developed had the series not been cancelled.

The East

Similarities with *The OA* can also be identified in Marling and Batmanglij's second feature-length collaboration, the 2013 corporate espionage thriller *The East*, again written by the two, directed by Batmanglij, and starring Marling. Devoid of the (potentially) fantastic elements of its predecessor, *The East* sees Marlin in the role of Sarah, an investigator for a private intelligence firm tasked with infiltrating an anarchist cell – 'The East' of the film's title – which has been targeting multinational corporations. In addition to sharing the theme of infiltration of a secretive group with *Sound of My Voice* (the cell displays cult-like tendencies as shown in a ritualised communal dinner and their use of psychologically charged trust-building games which require members to divulge personal secrets to the group, something Maggie also demands), The East recalls the Crestwood group, as do the modern-day hobos Sarah encounters while freight hopping undercover to establish her identity as a societal drop-out and to establish contact with The East. Both the members of The East and these itinerants (whose joyous performance of folk songs using traditional acoustic instruments recalls Maggie's description of 2054 in which the culture industry no longer exists but an authentic folk culture flourishes) have embraced an 'alternative' lifestyle which rejects the conventions of modern society. Prairie's followers are similarly in search of an alternative mode of living which will provide their lives with meaning even if, as with Steve and French, they are initially in denial that this is the case. Joining Prairie's group gives a sense of *purpose* to their lives, as it does to those of the other three members. Although Sarah does have a degree of purpose in *The East*, provided by her job, she nevertheless comes to recognize her life before encountering the anarchists as lacking in meaning.

CONSTELLATIONS

Another Earth

Although it did not involve Batmanglij, *Another Earth* (2011), the feature film Marling starred in and co-wrote with its director, Mike Cahill, is also useful to consider in comparison to *The OA* as it too engages with the theme of an alternative life, albeit of a different type. The film uses the 'many worlds' trope from the science fiction and fantasy genres – as does *The OA*; see Chapter 3 – to represent the life lost to Rhoda, a promising high school student accepted to MIT, after she drives drunk, killing a pregnant, married woman and her young son as a result. In the film a 'mirror' version of the Earth arrives in the solar system, ultimately leading to an encounter by Rhoda with her counterpart from there who appears to have had the prosperous life Rhoda's earlier actions have prevented her from achieving. This encounter anticipates the events of the second season of *The OA* in which Prairie's claims about inter-dimensional travel and the existence of a 'multiverse' of parallel earths, populated by counterparts of the characters from season one, is revealed to be true. A significant difference, however, is that in *The OA*, characters engage with their inter-dimensional counterpart only after dying in their universe of origin or performing the five movements learned from NDEs, after which they can take over the counterpart's body on a parallel earth. In season two of *The OA* Prairie is able to experience a life she could have had if one event in her childhood had not occurred and she too had grown up to become prosperous, which I discuss in further detail in Chapter 3.

The many worlds trope is central to the story 'The Garden of Forking Paths' (1941) by the Argentinian fantasy writer Jorge Luis Borges. The story lends its title to the sixth episode of *The OA*'s first season ('Forking Paths'), in which it is used by Hap to describe the multiverse. In this episode, Hap realises that NDEs provide glimpses of parallel earths, rather than of 'the after-life'. The existence of the multiverse also brings *The OA* into the sub-genre of alternative history or 'what-if?' fiction when, in the first episode of season two, Prairie jumps, at the moment of her death, as shown in the season one finale, into the body of her counterpart in a universe where Joe Biden, rather than Barack Obama, is president of the United States in 2016. Although this element of the world Prairie has entered is not developed subsequently, it can read as a satirical comment on the mobilisation of racist Americans, outraged by Obama's presidency, into a network in support of Donald Trump, who won the

2016 presidential campaign, taking power in 2017. Biden's presence in the White House implies that such a mobilisation would not have taken place and presents an alternative history for the US resulting from this point of divergence from actual-world history. Similarly, the arrival of the duplicate world in *Another Earth* presents an alternative history for and to Rhoda, one in which she has fulfilled her earlier promise. As mentioned above, I discuss this facet of *The OA* further in Chapter 3, in the section on *The OA* as a 'multiversal' fiction.

Having established the *auterism* of Marling and Batmanglij in this chapter by identifying consistent narrative themes, diegetic techniques and production practices in their body of work so far, I will now discuss *The OA* in the context of the streaming of serialised drama facilitated by platforms such as Netflix and their various competitors. In doing so, I will address how the uploading of both seasons of the series in their entirety – a practice known as 'dumping' – relates to the *auteurism* discussed in this chapter, as well as the consumption of *The OA* by an audience able to control the flow of the narrative.

Chapter 2: *The OA* as a Streaming Serialised Drama

The New 'New Hollywood' and Prestige Television

Figure 2: Hap in his lair.

Although, as I argue below, *The OA* contains implied criticisms of the digital age, it is nevertheless difficult to conceive of *The OA* being produced in any other context than that of the current climate in which television is no longer perceived as an inferior medium to cinema but instead as a source of high quality or 'prestige' serial drama often featuring 'A-list' cinema actors and directors. This type of TV production can be traced back to the 'quality television' of MTM (as I discuss further below.) Nor is it easy to think of a studio other than Netflix Originals allowing Marling and Batmanglij the creative freedom they enjoyed with *The OA*. However, this very freedom has been identified as damaging to Marling and Batmanglij's efficacy as storytellers: Sean Hutchinson of online magazine *Inverse* has compared *The OA* unfavourably to *Sound of My Voice*, finding the film to be more focused and arguing that the series shows the two 'needed the budgetary and time restraints of independent movie making' and that Marling's centrality to *The OA*'s 16 episodes – she is in all but one – in fact 'detracts from her charismatic and slightly dangerous cult-like charm' (2017). Hutchinson's criticism of *The OA* as being cluttered with under-developed ideas – he argues that what he identifies as *The OA*'s 'excesses' resulted 'solely from what happens when independent film-makers suddenly find themselves with all of Netflix's resources at their disposal and the belief that they should put everything out there' – is echoed by *Guardian* journalist Jack Seale's dismissal of *The OA* as 'hokey bunkum' in which '[e]vents, characters and half-formed ideas are thrown at the screen then abandoned in favour of fresh mysteries, the show infinitely rolling out a carpet of kookiness' (2019). Like Hutchinson, Seale acknowledges the series' high production values, calling it 'rubbish, but handsomely mounted rubbish' and singling Batmanglij's 'dark flair' as a director out for praise while also naming him a 'casualty' of what he also sees as a lack of focus in *The OA*'s scripts.

Hutchinson compares Netflix's indulgence of series creators such as Marling and Batmanglij to the 'New Hollywood of the 1970s and '80s' (2017), an era in which, as documented by Peter Biskind in *Easy Riders, Raging Bulls: How the Sex-Drugs and Rock 'N Roll Generation Saved Hollywood* (1998), maverick directors such as William Friedkin, Francis Ford Coppola and Martin Scorsese were given comparable creative freedom by established Hollywood studios such as United Artists and Paramount Pictures, and produced innovative, and critically and commercially successful, films, now considered to be classics such as *The French Connection* (1971), *The Godfather* (1972) and *Taxi Driver* (1976). However, the 'New Hollywood' ultimately imploded because, as Hutchinson puts it, 'the very privilege allotted to film-makers bred a certain excess that led to diminishing quality'. He goes on to speculate that the 'same cracks might be beginning to show in Netflix's method' (2017), citing *The OA* as a specific example of excess. However, another example of an established media corporation providing creators unprecedented artistic freedom can be deployed as a useful point of comparison to Netflix, that of DC Comics' 'mature readers' imprint Vertigo, founded by editor Karen Berger in 1993 and discontinued in 2020. As well as publishing new titles, Vertigo also absorbed the existing DC series *Shade the Changing Man*; *Hellblazer*; *Animal Man*; *Swamp Thing*; *The Sandman*; and *Doom Patrol*, continuing their existing issue numbering and, in all cases except that of *Swamp Thing*, retaining their writers. Under Berger, these series severed their ties to the continuity of the shared fictional world of the 'DC Universe' and their writers were allowed, even encouraged, to produce experimental narratives without the same commercial or editorial pressures of the main line of DC's superhero titles.

Although some Vertigo series were commercially successful – most notably *The Sandman* (1989-1996, adapted to television by Netflix in 2022) and *Preacher* (1995-2000; adapted to television by AMC in 2016) – Berger also allowed less popular series to continue for longer than would have usually been the case for an under-performing DC title. This was the case with *The Invisibles* (1994-2000) a highly innovative comic created by writer Grant Morrison which shares some similarities with *The OA* in its mystical themes and use of meta-fictional tropes – specifically, metalepsis, the presentation of a narrative within a narrative as occurs in several issues of the comic, including the fifth issue of the second volume (1997) in which a character reads a previous issue, remarking that the author is 'making this too far-fetched' – and which is also characterised by an abundance of ideas. Netflix has not been quite so indulgent, cancelling *The OA* after two seasons as was also the fate of another Originals production with which it shares some thematic concerns, *Sense8*, produced by the Wachowskis, best known for the 1999 Gnostic science fiction film *The Matrix* and its sequels (which also bear strong similarities with *The Invisibles* thematically and visually). Nevertheless, that both series were produced at all is indicative of a willingness to experiment with the form of television comparable to Vertigo's innovations in the field of comics. Furthermore, the decision by Netflix to make entire seasons of *The OA*, and other series, available to view all at once recalls Vertigo's promotion of collected issues of comic series as 'graphic novels', which presented an alternative method of consuming comics to that offered by monthly publication schedules. The availability of these collected editions in bookshops as well as specialist comic book retailers was also a major factor in increasing the acceptability of comics as a 'valid' or 'legitimate' medium comparable to the literary novel in America and the UK in the 1980s and '90s.

Similarly, the high production values and narrative complexity of 'prestige' TV series has seen them compared to cinematic productions (to the extent that the British Film Institute's magazine *Sight & Sound* included *Twin Peaks: The Return* in its top films of 2017 poll, prompting a heated discussion in its letters page over what constitutes a 'film' in the digital age. Peter Debruge (2016), chief film critic of *Variety*, referred to *The OA* as one of the 'most important films' of 2016; in addition to Batmanglij, directors on the second season include the arthouse film-makers Andrew Haigh

(*45 Years* [2015]) and Anna Rose Holmer (*The Fits* [2015]), while the screenwriter Henry Bean (*The Believer* [2001]) co-wrote episodes five and seven of season two with Marling. Indeed, it has been suggested by some fans that both *Sense8* and *The OA* could be continued in comic form as has already been the case for the cancelled TV series *Buffy the Vampire Slayer* (1997-2004; directly continued in comics from 2007-2018) and *Jericho* (2006-2008; continued as a comic 2009-2012). However, the 'freedom' provided by the comic book medium, and its removal of budgetary limitations, has its own dangers, or what Hutchinson would call 'traps', as acknowledged by *Buffy* creator Joss Whedon after some fans complained, online and in the comic's letters page, that he and his writing staff has lost focus with the first 'season' of the comic book continuation of the series, which seemed to prioritise visual spectacle impossible to realise on a television budget over the characterisation central to the show's appeal for many fans. Operating on a significantly higher budget than *Buffy* ever did, *The OA* has already received, as we have seen, similar criticism from Hutchinson and Seale, among others, as a television series; neither Marling nor Batmanglij has a professional background in comics (unlike the Wachowksis, who have written comics professionally, and co-creator of *Sense8* J. Michael Straczynski) so adapting the series to comics could indeed lead them into a similar 'trap' of artistic freedom.

It is perhaps worth noting here too that Netflix entered into comic book publishing following its 2017 deal with the highly successful comic writer (and former Grant Morrison collaborator) Mark Millar to produce his comics and adapt them as Originals series. Millar has also compared Netflix to Hollywood, albeit to a different era – that of the 1920s when studios produced weekly serials as well as feature films (Viscardi, 2018). Like the serials of the Hollywood era Millar mentions, comic series maintain audience interest through narrative suspense, particularly in the use of cliffhanger endings to individual episodes or issues. In his study of serial TV, including streaming platforms such as Netflix, *Birth of the Binge*, Dennis Broe argues that serialised television since the 'dawn of the Reagan years and the birth of neoliberalism' (2019: 1) in the early 1980s 'engages addiction directly in its acceleration of older narrative tropes' including the traditional cliffhanger ending which 'becomes the multicharacter cliffhanger' (3). This is certainly the case with *The OA*: although Prairie is its main protagonist – to its detriment, as far as Hutchinson is concerned – the Crestwood group are nevertheless also central to the series, providing multiple identification figures to its audience as well as valuable assistance to Prairie. Indeed, Marling has written, in a statement posted on Twitter after the cancellation of the series, about her and Batmanglij's desire to create 'stories that illustrate the power of collective protagonism rather than focusing on a traditional, singular heroic figure' (2019). In the statement, Marling also relates an anecdote about meeting a fan protesting the cancellation on a Hollywood street holding a hunger strike: the fan told her 'what I'm really protesting is late capitalism'. The fan then said something Marling claims she has not 'been able to forget since': 'Algorithms are not as smart as we are. They cannot account for love.' Marling uses similar language earlier in the statement, writing that *The OA* was a casualty of 'late capitalism's push toward consolidation and economies of scale'. Marling seems to forget here that *The OA*'s existence was a direct result of Netflix's domination of the market for streamed serial TV which is very much a product of 'late capitalism'. She overlooks too that 'multiple protagonism' is an already established aspect not only of soap operas but also of 'quality television' as in, for example, the ensemble casts of the American police series *Hill Street Blues* (1981-1987), an example Broe cites, or, more recently HBO's *The Wire* (2002-2008) and the supporting characters who assist the eponymous hero of *Buffy the Vampire Slayer*, known to fans as the 'Scooby Gang', as well as featuring in their own sub-plots (and, in some cases, 'starring' in spin-off comic books).

Current 'prestige' TV, like *The OA*, can be considered as a development of the 'quality television' pioneered in the US by the independent production company MTM Enterprises (see Feuer, Kerr and Vahimagi, 1984), established in 1969, which produced such notable series as *Lou Grant* (1977-1982); *Hill Street Blues*; and *St Elsewhere* (1982-1988). 'Quality' television drama tended to focus on realism, avoiding such 'marginalized' genres, as Lacy Hodges describes them (2008: 231), as science fiction and horror; however, this would change in the early 1990s with the success of *The X-Files* (1993-2018), a series which became a global popular culture phenomenon. Hodges describes *The X-Files* as a 'hybrid' series which 'incorporates tropes from many genres both mainstream (detective fiction and police procedurals) and marginalized (science fiction and horror)' which allows it to 'occupy a liminal space between the mainstream and the margins' resulting in a 'success that was previously unavailable to most science fiction shows' (231). She also identifies the short-lived and briefly popular series *Twin Peaks* (1990-1991), created by Mark Frost and David Lynch as one of the 'key antecedents' for *The X-Files* and explains its relative failure as a result of its inability to 'conform to mainstream televisual aesthetics and narrative structures' (232). *The X-Files* had no such difficulty, managing to effectively combine shared thematic concerns with *Twin Peaks* with what Robin Nelson terms 'critical realism': 'realism that constructs fictional narratives based on specific aspects of the historical world' (Nelson, 1997: 113). For Hodges, the success of *The X-Files* paved the way for the production of the ABC science fiction/horror series *Lost* (2004-2010), which approached *The X-Files*' popularity (231); in turn, *Lost*'s success is responsible for creating an audience receptive to series such as not only *The OA*, but also *The Leftovers* (2014-2017), co-created by *Lost*'s co-creator Damon Lindelof, and *True Detective* (2017-2019) both of which were produced by HBO, the American pay television channel established in 1972 which has taken on MTM's mantle as the premier producer of quality/prestige television. Like *Lost*, these HBO series combined elements of genres hitherto considered 'marginalized' with both 'critical realism' and innovative narrative techniques, in part influenced by filmmakers such as Lynch. This was also the case with *The OA* although, as the criticisms by Hutchinson and Seale noted above suggest, *The OA*'s failure can be attributed to a deviation from conventional structures, even those of *Lost* and its successors, that has been identified as a lack of focus, an accusation also raised against *Twin Peaks*, particularly in its second season (Hodges, 2008: 233).

Media Technology and 'Post Cinematic Affect' in *The OA*

Media technology – including digital streaming – is of central thematic importance to *The OA* and its own 'critical realism'. The opening scene of the first episode is of phone camera footage – shown in an aspect ratio resembling the rectangle of a smartphone screen – showing Prairie about to jump from a bridge in St Louis into the river below. This footage – in which Prairie, in a long dress, resembles the photograph of Maggie that Carol shows Lorna in *Sound of My Voice* – is later posted on YouTube, under the title 'Homeless Woman Jumps Off Bridge' and is how Nancy (Alice Krige) and Abel (Scott Wilson), Prairie's adoptive parents, learn of her reappearance. When Nancy and Abel collect her from hospital and return her to the family home in Crestwood, Michigan, Prairie is subsequently shown with a video camera recording a message to Homer, a fellow former captive of Hap, which Nancy later watches without her permission. Prairie also has the camera with her the first time she encounters the four boys who will become members of her group – Steve, Jesse, French and Buck – in the unfinished house in their neighbourhood out of which Steve and Jesse deal drugs. Steve is enraged by Prairie's intrusion into his place of business because he believes she is filming him there and also because her return has brought into his territory a news media presence which could potentially expose his criminal activities. Steve snatches the camera from Prairie and when she attempts to take it back sets his dog Axel on her. Prairie struggles with and ultimately subdues the dog by biting it – an expression of the lupine aspect of her spirit as also represented by the sweatshirt emblazoned with a wolf's head she wears later in the series, including in the first season finale – much to the astonishment of the four boys, which Jesse films on his phone.

Filming appears to be an activity central to Jesse's life: in their first appearance in the series, earlier in the episode, Jesse is shown filming Steve perform stunts on the roof of the unfinished house; later in the episode Steve informs Prairie that he and Jesse have a YouTube channel which Steve intends to use to promote his services as a fitness trainer, particularly for celebrities. From the roof they notice Prairie and her adoptive mother Nancy out walking and Jesse turns the camera on them as they pass by. When Steve is later having sex with Jaye (Shannon Walsh), a girl from his school, he looks at a paused image of Prairie from this footage on his laptop screen, indicating his developing desire for her; as Jaye gets dressed afterwards, Steve asks her to get into bed with him and watch 'stuff' on his laptop – a reference, perhaps, to the popular euphemism for casual sex, 'Netflix and chill' – an offer she declines, telling him that her interest in him is purely physical, rather than romantic, as Steve seems to want, and that their relationship 'isn't a thing'. Steve responds by saying that he is 'into someone else' who, given that he is looking at the laptop as he speaks, the viewer takes to be Prairie.

Prairie goes to the abandoned house in search of a Wi-Fi password as she is unable to get online at home because Nancy and Abel are restricting her phone and internet use following advice from the hospital in St Louis where Prairie was taken after the bridge incident. Frustrated at this literal disconnection, Prairie wanders the neighbourhood, eventually coming upon the unfinished house and encountering French, who is waiting in line to buy drugs from Steve. She asks French for his Wi-Fi password, or that of a neighbour, but he directs her towards Steve instead. Prairie's disconnection from networked communications is represented by her carrying the camera, rather than a phone, which also symbolises her separation from the rest of the neighbourhood, including her parents, and from society in general, emphasising her Otherness.

Recording technology is also associated with Prairie in the form of the video tapes of her speaking Russian in her sleep as a child made by her adoptive parents which she comes across in their home office, offering the first hint to the viewer of this aspect of her mysterious past. The office also houses their files of newspaper clippings pertaining to Prairie's disappearance. This 'old media' archive demonstrates the extent of their love for Prairie and the devastating impact her disappearance had on them. Old media, in the form of TV, also indicates an actual world influence on *The OA*: as she slips out to find a Wi-Fi password, Prairie passes a television broadcasting a documentary about Elizabeth Smart, who was abducted from her Salt Lake City home at the age of 14 in 2002. 'Can this girl go back to being a normal individual?' the presenter asks, a question which is, of course, also relevant to Prairie, although it is debatable if she has ever been 'normal' at all. (I discuss the influence of Smart's abduction on *The OA* further in Chapter 4.)

The prominence of media technology in the series is part of its realism in representing the, to use Steven Shaviro's term, 'post cinematic affect' of modern America to which networked communication and recording devices with screens are central (as is archived media; significantly, Steve gets his idea to help Prairie from the classic film noir *Strangers on a Train* [1951]) and which is composed, as Shaviro has observed, 'as much of things that happen on screens or in optical cables as of things that we can see and touch directly' (2011). Furthermore, the importance of streamed footage in the first episode, and from the opening scene, also draws attention to *The*

OA's status as a Netflix Originals production designed to be consumed *online*. Like most other Netflix Originals, the entirety of both seasons of *The OA* was uploaded at once to the Netflix platform, providing viewers with the opportunity to 'binge watch' the whole season in one sitting. Netflix also offers viewers a high degree of control over consumption of the narrative, including the ability to pause, fast forward and rewind at will.

This level of control can play a key factor in the interpretation of *The OA*, which is laden with symbolism, allusions and foreshadowing: for example, the reference to Elizabeth Smart's abduction mentioned above points the interested viewer towards that event, to which the claim of being angelic was key (see Chapter 4), even though it is referred to only briefly and as background noise, so is easily overlooked. Another example, from the second episode of season one, is the presence, in a flashback, to Prairie's childhood before she was adopted by Nancy and Abel – Russian dolls in the brothel Prairie, then known as Nina, lives in with her aunt following her father's death. As I discuss in Chapter 3, these dolls are symbolic of the series' thematic status as a *multiversal* fiction. As with the reference to Smart, the dolls are shown only briefly and with no particular importance explicitly attributed to them in-scene, so their significance could go unnoticed on a first viewing. Nancy opens the dolls up just before she first encounters Nina, and makes the decision to adopt her: the dolls can be interpreted, therefore, as symbolising, and foreshadowing, the layered multiverse which Nina will navigate as The OA which is made explicit when Hap uses them to illustrate the ways in which inter-dimensional travellers take over their counterparts' bodies to Prairie in the second episode of season two. They also symbolise Nancy's, and Abel's, entry into the layers of Nina's past: after they catch her sleep-walking with a knife later in episode two, the adoptive parents send Nina, now known as Prairie, to a psychologist who tells them that she is spinning 'tales of grandeur that she believes are reality'. This foreshadows French's discovery of the books in Prairie's room in the season one finale in a scene in which dolls are also present, albeit not of the Russian variety, which French briefly investigates just before he finds the books, suggesting both to him and to the viewer the possibility that the adult Prairie may be an unreliable narrator. Nina's aunt does not give Nancy and Abel any background information on her and also warns them to keep her provenance a secret. As all the information about Prairie's origins the viewer receives come directly from her, the veracity of her claims – and therefore her status as a trustworthy narrator – is problematised here: like her group, the viewer is simultaneously enthralled by the tale (and the teller) while sceptical about its truth.

The Russian dolls in the flashback, and those in the scene where French is in Prairie's bedroom, are themselves foreshadowed in the scene from the first episode in which Prairie films a dollhouse with her video camera before using it to record herself speaking to Homer. An image of reduction and containment, the dollhouse prefigures both the abandoned home where Prairie will tell her story, and the captivity of Hap's prisoners and their status as his playthings. The artificiality of the dollhouse also anticipates the miniature model structures revealed in the final episode of season two, which throws the reality of all previous episodes in to question, as I discuss further in Chapter 3, in the section on *The OA* and Gnosticism, and in Chapter 5 in relation to certain episodes of *The Twilight Zone*. The dolls, and Prairie's Russian origins, are perhaps also an allusion to Nabokov's *Pale Fire* (see previous chapter), a novel which is also concerned with multiplicity and layering and which, as a narrative of, in Brian McHale's words, 'absolute epistemological uncertainty' (much like *The OA* itself) encourages re-reading in order to uncover clues as to the 'true' identity of its narrator. *The OA* also encourages, and rewards, re-viewing (which Netflix facilitates) as evidenced by discussions on forums dedicated to the series on sites such as Reddit and MovieChat as well as social media platforms like Facebook and Twitter. As with re-reading, re-viewing allows the consumer of a work of fiction to shift their focus away from the resolution of narrative suspense – because they already know what happens in the story – and on to the *texture* of the fictional world presented in the narrative, as constructed from details which may be overlooked on a first reading or viewing. Subsequent recognition of these details can enhance the reading/viewing experience – what Roland Barthes, an avid re-reader, called the 'pleasure of the text' in his 1973 book of that title – particularly when engaging with a mystery like that presented by *The OA* or a comparable series such as the highly enigmatic and symbol-rich *Twin Peaks*. Both series have a dedicated fan base, members of which engage in practices of re-reviewing as creative acts of interpretation. *Twin Peaks* of course pre-dates the rise of online streaming services but home video recordings of episodes allowed a level of narrative control approaching that of platforms like Netflix for viewers in the pre-digital age, allowing them to re-watch the series in an attempt to understand and explain it. The series' third season, presented by the network Showtime under the title *Twin Peaks: The Return*, was released in 2017, both on television and via online streaming, offering control of its narrative equivalent to that provided by Netflix.

When Prairie eventually does achieve internet access in episode one – provided by Steve after she impersonates his mother in a meeting with BBA in order to prevent his expulsion from school, a performance which prefigures the metafictional revelations of the season two finale in which Marling plays a version of herself playing a character in a TV show which resembles *The OA*, as does Prairie's use of a theatrical metaphor to describe BBA's relationship with Steve, as I discuss further in Chapter 5 – she immediately searches YouTube for footage of Homer, a star college football quarterback who experienced an NDE after an accident during a game. Earlier in the episode, while filming a message to Homer, Prairie had admitted 'there are moments when I think I made you up': as with Maggie's use of the song 'Dreams' by The Cranberries as 'proof' of her claim to be a time traveller from the future in *Sound of My Voice* (see Chapter 1), Prairie's admission, combined with the television news report about Homer she watches on YouTube, calls into question, for the viewer, the veracity of the story she later tells the Crestwood group. Like 'Dreams' as used by Maggie, the footage appears to simply be 'real world' source material for Prairie's story, much as the Elizabeth Smart abduction is for Marling and Batmanglij (and as clips from a variety of media, including the films *Orphee* by Jean Cocteau [1950], Guy Green's *A Patch of Blue* [1965] and *The Descent* [2005] by Neil Marshall, along with fragments of a furniture advert, a game show and a children's programme are for Rachel in the televisual collage she uses to explain Prairie's situation to the Crestwood group in episode three of season two). This interpretation becomes particularly persuasive after French discovers the books hidden in Prairie's bedroom in the first season finale, which also appear to be sources of material for her tale.

After watching the footage, Prairie begins to sob and to speak to Homer, pleading to know his whereabouts: this moment can be interpreted as representing Prairie as a fantasist rather than a maker of fiction, the significant difference being that Prairie seems to believe her own inventions even if she occasionally doubts them. If Prairie is using the lives of others as the basis for her story, her actions are similar to those of Angela Wesselman who, as recounted in the documentary film *Catfish* (2010), used images of other people to create multiple social media accounts, one of which she deployed to create a relationship with the film's subject, photographer Nev Shulman. Wesselman subsequently used the accounts to convince Schulman of the existence of a large extended family which she had entirely invented. Significantly, the directors of *Catfish*, Henry Joost and Schulman's brother Ariel, went on to make the third and fourth entries in the *Paranormal Activity* series of 'found footage' horror films (2007–), to which media technology, and the appearance of realism, are central narrative components. Prairie also appears to use 'found footage' (and text) throughout the first season, the ambiguity of the season finale notwithstanding. Regardless of whether or not she is lying about her experiences in captivity, *The OA*, like *Catfish*, represents the way in which the internet functions as a media archive: technology journalist Virginia Heffernan has gone so far as to state that 'internet video is our ranking realist form, it *is* history' (2016: 134; original emphasis). The realistic (because true) and historical qualities (again, because it actually happened, within the world of the series) of the YouTube clip Prairie watches of Homer are recombined into her fantasy. Unless, that is, she is telling the truth in which case her doubts over her memories of being imprisoned with Homer may be symptoms of post-traumatic stress. The beginning of season two suggests that Prairie has been sincere all along; although, as previously observed, the events of the second season finale throw all previous events into question, as I discuss further throughout this study of the series.

'The Visible You'

Internet video allows for, and encourages, the presentation of what Prairie calls the 'visible you': one's physical self and personality, as displayed online through video sites like YouTube and Vimeo, and on social media platforms such as Facebook and Instagram. Steve is preoccupied with his visible presentation, hence his interest in both physical fitness and celebrity, but his rejection by Jaye – who acknowledges he has a 'really nice body' just before she informs him their relationship 'isn't a thing' – seems motivated by what she perceives as a lack of depth in him. Jaye instead prefers Miles, a star singer in the school's choir who, as such, is richer in cultural capital than Steve and more interesting to Jaye as a result. The contrast between the two boys presents Steve as superficial and vain, lacking in genuine talent much like the stars of reality television and social media 'influencers' – for example, the Kardashians – who are often criticised as 'being famous for being famous' but are just the kind of celebrities Steve desires as clients for his physical fitness training services. Steve informs Prairie of his ambitions in this direction in the first episode after telling her about Jaye's rejection of him. Prairie acknowledges that Steve's 'visible you' is 'impressive' but criticises him for prioritising his physicality at the expense of developing his 'invisible self' by which she means 'longings... the desires you don't tell anyone about' (the phrase 'invisible self' is also the title of the first season finale). Steve argues that his ambitions to be a trainer, and also a celebrity himself by presenting his own fitness show, do constitute his invisible self but Prairie dismisses these desires as further expressions of his 'visible you'. Although he initially responds to this criticism angrily – calling Prairie 'crazy' – Steve then asks for advice on developing his invisible self. Prairie tells him to begin by closing his eyes, which she compares to her own earlier blindness, a state which caused others to underestimate her and which she considers to have been 'powerful' because it 'made me listen'. Steve tries closing his eyes, in a state of voluntary disconnection from the visible world, but quickly finds the experience 'boring' suggesting a dependence on visual stimulation already indicated in his earlier sexual intercourse with Jaye during which he looks at an image of Prairie and after which he asks her to watch online media with him (Jaye also later reveals that Steve likes to look at himself when they have sex). Prairie's request that Steve close his eyes can be interpreted as the beginning of her initiation of him into her group where the 'new media' of networked digital devices will be replaced by a focus on perhaps the oldest medium, that of the voice. Nevertheless, the Crestwood group assemble via social media after Prairie posts a video asking for help on YouTube just before her internet access is taken away and her camera confiscated by her parents as punishment for impersonating Steve's mother. Prairie instructs them all to close their eyes before she begins her tale, which not only focuses their concentration but further disconnects them from the networked world and its preponderance of screens, the source of Shaviro's 'post cinematic affect'.

Stranger Things

In her 2020 essay for *The New York Times*, Marling also spoke of her hopes for stories with *no* protagonist, which is perhaps how *The OA* would have developed had it not been cancelled.

Looking again towards comics, perhaps one model for 'multiple protagonism' which does not involve a team orbiting a central exceptional figure is the mini-series *Global Frequency* [2002-2004], created and written by Warren Ellis, illustrated by several artists, and inspired by smart mobs: groups of like-minded individuals geographically distant but connected by digital technology. The comic concerns the organisation of its title which responds to emergencies and crises by 'activating' its covert members as and when required and according to their specialist skills and abilities. Each individual issue focuses on one of these individuals. The only recurring characters are the head of Global Frequency, Miranda Zero, and Aleph, the organisation's mission dispatcher, whose name is a reference to the title of the Borges short story 'The Aleph' (1945). Neither Zero nor Aleph resemble a conventional protagonist. The series was optioned for television and a pilot produced although unaired.

Multiple protagonism is also a key feature of another Netflix Originals production, *Stranger Things* (2016-), perhaps the platform's most successful original production to date.[2] As with *The OA*, *Stranger Things* involves a group of high school boys forming a group around a female, Eleven, with a fantastic background as a captive who has been experimented upon; and, like *The OA*, *Stranger Things* also represents inter-dimensional travel, to the realm of the 'Upside Down', a sort of dark aspect of the collective unconscious (which is mentioned by the character Yassi [Sheila Vand] in the fourth episode of season two of *The OA*). Set in the Reaganite USA of the 1980s, and deeply nostalgic for, and heavily laden with, references to the popular culture of that era, the second and third seasons of the series saw a lightening of tone compared to the first and an increased emphasis on these elements of pop culture reference and homage. The tonally darker first season, which offered a more complex and critical representation of Reagan's America, particularly the activities of the intelligence services in the context of the Cold War, bears strong similarities to the 2010 science fiction/horror film *Beyond the Black Rainbow*, set in 1983 and directed and written by Panos Cosmatos (perhaps better known for his subsequent feature *Mandy* [2018] starring Nicolas Cage). *Beyond the Black Rainbow* also shares some common elements with *The OA* in its depiction of scientific experimentation on a young woman being undertaken by an obsessive male scientist in pursuit of transcendence of the material plane. As with both seasons of *The OA*, Netflix released each of the three seasons of *Stranger Things* in their entirety in 2016, 2017 and 2019 respectively. A fourth season is scheduled for release in 2022. The first two seasons were also subsequently released as limited edition DVD and Blu-ray box-sets, the year after their initial streaming, in packaging imitating VHS video cassettes, consistent with the series' emphasis on nostalgia. At the time of writing *The OA* remains available only via streaming on Netflix which is perhaps an indication of its relative lack of success, although with its cult following there would undoubtedly be a market for it in physical form (including the current author).

'Keep Them Watching'

Writing in the April 2019 issue of *Sight & Sound*, James Bell argues that 'Keep them watching...' could be Netflix's 'motto' (27). Bell notes that the 'production of original "content" is key to the dominance of the streaming giants' of which Netflix is one, along with, among others, Amazon Prime, Hulu and Apple TV. According to Bell, Netflix now produces 'more original content than any television network in history' (27), a statement which is all the more remarkable given that the company has only been doing so since 2012 with the release of the mobster-out-of-water series *Lilyhammer* (2012-2015) starring Steven Van Zandt in a role similar to the one he played in the HBO series *The Sopranos* (1999-2007), the critical success of which was a key factor in creating a market for similarly 'complex', and high budget, television series. Bell identifies Netflix's acquisition of the rights to produce film director David

Fincher's remake of the BBC television series *House of Cards* (1990, adapted from the novel by Michael Dibbs published a year earlier) as the 'game changer' for streamed TV, not so much for its content as for Netflix's decision to release the first season (2013) in its entirety, a 'release strategy for the show that really shook up tried-and-tested models' (27). This act of 'dumping' by Netflix replaced the conventional model in which a network would 'drip-feed' viewers new episodes, relying on the suspense created by cliffhanger endings to entice audiences to return on a weekly basis (as had also been the case with the film serials of the 1920s referred to by Mark Millar following his development and publishing deal with Netflix, discussed above). Dumping recreates the experience of consuming box-sets, which had become increasingly popular in the 1990s and 2000s, to the extent that, as Bell observes, the term 'box-set' is now used by streaming platforms to describe dumped series 'despite there no longer being a physical object to speak of' (27). The 'boxing' of a TV series into a 'set' of video cassettes or digital discs recalls the compilation of single, saddle-stitched issues of a comic book series into book form, complete with a spine and an ISBN, which is commonly known as a 'graphic novel', discussed above. The term is often something of a misnomer as collected volumes of series such as *The Invisibles* or *The Sandman*, referred to in the comic book industry as 'trade paperbacks' and by readers as 'trades', usually consist of individual story-arcs (which are structured by creators with this kind of compilation in mind) rather than the entirety of the series. Nevertheless, just as the presence of a spine and an ISBN makes the collected issues suitable for retail in a bookshop, so the status of the 'novel' lends a certain perceived respectability to the comic book form. TV series such as *The Sopranos* or *House of Cards*, which, like *Stranger Things*, has been released on DVD and Blu-ray, are often discussed in comparison to 'novels' in terms of their perceived similarities in complexity and sophistication – even though there is nothing inherently complex or sophisticated about the form of the novel – and the ownership of them in box-set form which can be shelved, reinforces this notion of the 'prestige' TV series as the modern equivalent of the literary novel. Of course, novels themselves were often serialised in chapter form in the nineteenth and early twentieth centuries, as in the cases of Arthur Conan Doyle or Charles Dickens. Batmanglij has spoken of the latter's serialised fiction as a model he and Marling had considered imitating for the release of *Sound of My Voice* as a web-series had it not achieved studio distribution (Chang, 2012), a practical solution to distribution which also subtly suggests that *The OA* is the contemporary equivalent of Dickens' work, just as the emulation of the VHS format in the packaging of *Stranger Things* box-sets places the series in a lineage with '80s pop culture. The association of *The OA* with literary fiction is also apparent in the titling of each episode as a 'chapter'.

Dumping imitates the box-set not only by presenting the viewer with a series in collected form but also in providing the viewer with the ability to re-watch specific episodes, wholly or in part, in whichever order they choose. As discussed above, *The OA*, with its rich symbolism and use of subtle foreshadowing, rewards, and encourages, such re-viewing. However, Broe argues that the perceived 'narrative complexity' of 'seriality' or 'Serial TV' – a phrase he equates with the industry term of 'Quality TV' as well as the critical term 'Complex TV' as coined by Jason Mitchell in his 2006 essay 'Narrative Complexity in Contemporary American Television' – may in fact 'simply be a duplication of technological complexity' in the wider world (1). Broe cites Theodor Adorno's comparison of 'the Fordist culture industry' to the industrial assembly line, characterised by the repetition of specialised labour, as a precedent for his own comparison of Serial TV and other 'hyperindustrial products in the era of the mobile computer' to the 'new virtual accumulation' central to contemporary capitalism (2-3). For Broe, 'capital has in many ways reached its capacity or continues to brush against its limits, in areas such as contamination of the planet and its exhaustion of sustainable energy'; under these conditions, 'the digital "virtual world" becomes capital's (sole?) hope and beacon for its promise of abundance and the site of its last pretensions to equality' (2). Serial TV is 'an integral part of that strained abundance' and the devices on which it is viewed a 'deadening imprint of the process of virtual accumulation' (2). Narrative complexity is primarily concerned, therefore, on 'tracking increasingly intricate but also highly repetitive patterns' instead of 'making sense of the world' (3).

We might compare Broe's description of seriality to *Telegraph* critic Ed Power's assessment that *The OA* 'truly comes into its own when you stop attempting to piece together the storyline and instead submit to Marling and Batmanglij's vision' (2019). Surrendering to this vision does indeed involve a tracking of patterns in the form of the movements Prairie uses to travel inter-dimensionally, and which the Crestwood group deploy to distract the high school shooter at the end of season one, as well as the 'Q symphony' puzzle game featured in season two. However, in tracking these patterns viewers are able to make sense of, if not their own world, then of the world(s) of the series. Furthermore, that 'Q symphony' is the creation of the tech-billionaire Pierre Ruskin – modelled on real-world practitioners of 'virtual accumulation', Elon Musk, who co-founded PayPal, and EBay founder Pierre Omidyar – and that Ruskin uses the game as a crowdsourcing and resourcing tool, allows Marling and Batmanglij to draw attention to the same 'strained abundance' and 'pretensions to equality' which Broe identifies, perhaps even more so following *The OA*'s cancellation and Marling's statements regarding 'late capitalism' and 'consolidation'.

No less a prominent critic of corporate capitalism than Naomi Klein – author of *No Logo: Taking Aim at the Brand Bullies* (1999) – has professed her admiration for *The OA* stating that the series 'is actually about another world IMO' (2019a) and supporting Marling's call for multi-protagonist narratives with the comment, 'No more heroes... just all the power we can create and conjure, together' (2019b; original ellipsis). Marling and Klein appeared onstage together in 2017, during the latter's promotional tour for her book *No is Not Enough: Resisting Trump's Shock Politics and Winning the World We Need* (2017), the audio version of which was narrated by Marling. In response to a request from Marling to place Trump's policies in the context of *No Logo*'s critique of the ubiquity of corporate branding, Klein responded by identifying Trump as having become a 'hollow brand' since his hosting of the reality TV series *The Apprentice* between the years of 2004 and 2017, which Klein considers to be 'televised class warfare' with a brand identity of 'impunity through wealth' (French, 2017), a phrase which could equally be applied to both Ruskin in *The OA* and the actual world moguls after whom he is modelled. Marling then suggested a counter-narrative to the tendency identified by Klein amongst Trump's opponents towards a divisive emphasis on 'my crisis is bigger than your crisis': instead Marling proposed a 'new story' in which 'the people will save the people', anticipating the collective protagonism later proposed by her (French, 2017). This suggestion, and Marling's association with Klein, indicates that perhaps she viewed her involvement with Netflix as both a subversive and a revolutionary move in which a media corporation was used to spread an anti-corporate, collective message (Morrison attempted something similar with *The Invisibles* which, as a DC publication, was ultimately a product of the publisher's parent company, Warner Bros.). And she had every reason to believe that Netflix would allow her, and Batmanglij, to fulfil their vision for the series after Netflix's then Vice President of Original Series Cindy Holland released a statement ahead of season two, praising it and confirming *The OA* had been conceived from the outset as 'one long story' intended to be told over five seasons (Travers, 2018).

Such a bold narrative strategy of course requires a high degree of commitment from viewers, particularly given the heavy use of foreshadowing and world-building present in the series which have been misinterpreted as under-developed ideas, as discussed in the previous chapter. Phil Archbold (2019) has argued that the 'real reason' *The OA* was cancelled by Netflix was because it failed to attract new viewers, which Netflix's business model demands. For Archbold this is because, despite the 'teasing' elements of the narrative, which should make it 'binge-worthy', Marling and Batmanglij fail to answer many of the diegetic questions they raise, or do so with simply more questions, leaving all but the most committed viewers frustrated. As Archbold puts it: 'Netflix isn't going to continue to fund a show that loses people's interest before they get to the payoff' (2019); he quotes a review of *The OA* by Vinnie Mancuso for the *Observer* – entitled 'I Cannot Stop Laughing at *The OA*, Netflix's Very Serious Sci-Fi Series' – in which it is recommended that the series is best consumed 'in small doses' like 'crack cocaine'. Although intended to be humorous, Mancuso's remark is nevertheless indicative of a refusal to fully immerse himself in *The OA* which its nature as a streaming series – and one which is available in its entirety from the day of its release – facilitates. Doing so, and adjusting to a different form of 'teasing' narrative than the one Archbold claims viewers expect (which itself seems to be an old-fashioned model of TV consumption), and making full use of the capacity for control of the narrative that streaming provides, makes for a visual experience which is perhaps closer to reading a similarly layered and nuanced comic book narrative, rich in visual symbolism, such as *The Invisibles* or other titles released by Vertigo, than it is to conventional television viewing of the kind referred to by Archbold. That Marling and Batmanglij designate each season as a 'part' and individual episodes as 'chapters' – a technique common in Vertigo publications – is indicative of their intentions, and ambitions, for *The OA* to be approached as, in Cindy Holland's words, 'one long story' comparable to a graphic novel as much as – if not more so than – a literary one.

The OA and Critical Realism

Hodges argues that *The X-Files* is a more effective text of critical realism than *Twin Peaks* because it has a 'more concrete connection to the "real world" (2008: 233); as result, and because the series is 'willing to question and undermine dominant ideological structures within a consistently realist framework', *The X-Files* is, for Hodges, 'the most successful SFTV series to effectively explore the paranoia and confusion that dominates the post-WWII American cultural imaginary' (233-4). Similarly, *The OA* is extremely effective as a text of critical realism for a traumatised America following the financial crisis of 2008 and during the Trump era with its emphasis on 'fake news' and 'post-truth'; furthermore, it engages with the rise of digital technology and, correspondingly, of 'post cinematic affect', including the capacity for that technology to both isolate and connect individuals and to encourage them to value their 'visible you' over their 'invisible self'. 'Critical realism,' writes Nelson, 'shakes, if does not actually break, the TV drama's realist mould' (1997: 120); furthermore, it is the 'agent of the grotesque' (121) due to its potential for combining conventional realism with elements of Hodges' 'marginalized' genres. Far from lacking focus, or being over-burdened with undeveloped ideas, *The OA* uses the 'historical world' of post-2008/Trump-era America as the starting point for its own genre hybridization to represent affectively the reality of life in the second decade of the twenty-first century, as I discuss further in the next chapter.

Chapter 3: *The OA* and Genre

Figure 3: Karim Washington, PI.

Netflix categorises *The OA* generically as 'Sci Fi', 'Mystery', 'Thriller' and 'Drama', while IMDb classifies the series as 'Drama, Fantasy, Mystery', partly intersecting with Netflix's categorisations but removing thriller and replacing science fiction with fantasy as the indication of its non-realist elements. If *The OA* is to be considered science fiction it is certainly not of the 'hard' variety, i.e. texts characterised by a preoccupation with technological and scientific realism. Rather, *The OA* is closer to the work of Philip K. Dick – particularly his novels *The Man in the High Castle* (1962), *Flow My Tears, the Policeman Said* (1974), *VALIS* (1981), and its sequel *The Divine Invasion* (1981) – in its thematic concerns with mysticism and the nature of reality. It recalls too Grant Morrison's Vertigo comic book series *The Invisibles*, itself influenced by Dick, which displays similar themes, and also the Wachowskis' 1999 film *The Matrix* and its two sequels (2003), which in turn show an influence from Morrison (although the film-makers have never acknowledged the visual similarity between the characters from *The Matrix*, Neo and Morpheus, and King Mob from *The Invisibles* is undeniable). Like the work of Dick, Morrison and the Wachowskis, *The OA* can be described as a Gnostic text, that is, one which is concerned with the acquisition of spiritual knowledge which leads to an understanding of reality's true nature. This is an aspect of another Netflix Originals series, *Sense8* co-created by the Wachowskis with J. Michael Stracynski whose 'space opera' TV series *Babylon 5* (1993-97) also contained Gnostic themes. I discuss this aspect of *The OA* in further detail below. First, however, I will address the mystery and science fiction elements of the series as well as those from another genre not identified in either Netflix's or IMDb's classification: that of horror. I will conclude this section with a consideration of *The OA* as part of the emergent 'New Age' genre.

Mystery

The mystery in the first season of *The OA* comes from the possibility that Prairie is an unreliable narrator to her audience – and, by extension, to the viewer – and that she may, in fact, be a fantasist who, for the most part, believes her own delusions. This ambiguous status allows Marling and Batmanglij to explore in this season the themes of faith and belief also evident in their films *Sound of My Voice* and *The East*. They return to these themes in the second season with the fervent belief displayed in Prairie by Buck and Steve after her death at the hands of a high school shooter in the season one finale. French does not share this belief, however, particularly as it was he who discovered the books Prairie had apparently used as source material for her tale after breaking into her family home in the finale episode. French arranges to meet Abel, Prairie's father in the third episode of season two, who explains that the books were purchased on the advice of Prairie's counsellor as a therapeutic tool for her and that she had received them *after* she had started meeting with French and the others. French eventually recovers his faith in Prairie, while Jesse, who retains some doubts, as well as suffering from PTSD after the shooting, turns to opioids for relief and ultimately takes his own life with a deliberate overdose (season two, episode six).

With the enigma of Prairie's claims and history resolved for the viewer with Prairie's 'jump' to another dimension (and location, from Crestwood to San Francisco), in which she possesses the body of her counterpart in that dimension (Nina Azarova), mystery elements are introduced into the second season with the 'puzzle' that is the house in San Francisco's Nob Hill district and with the search for a missing girl (this dimension's version of Buck, who has not transitioned and still goes by the birth name Michelle Vu) by a new character, the private investigator Karim Washington (Kingsley Ben-Adir). Karim lives on a boat, which may be a comment on San Francisco's actual homelessness crisis which has seen residents set up homes on the waters around the city (Carlton, 2019). It also evokes an iconic boat-dwelling figure from American detective fiction, John D. MacDonald's Travis McGee, occupant of the Busted Flush, as well as the detectives Rick Simon and Sonny Crockett from, respectively, the TV series *Simon & Simon* (1981-1989) and *Miami Vice* (1984-1990), who both also live on the water. As Greg Taylor (2019) notes in his review of season two for the esoteric-themed website *The Daily Grail*, the presence of Karim allows Marling and Batmanglij to introduce elements of film noir to the series with the inclusion of 'the archetypes of the outsider private investigator and the damsel in distress leading him into danger and confusion'. Marling has been critical of noir for what she identifies as its inherent misogyny (2020) and so her encounter with the genre in a series centred around a female protagonist who does not conform to generic conventions can be interpreted as a critical engagement with it. There is a reference to a classic of film noir in episode two of the second season when Karim dons a pair of glasses and an affects an airy manner when he enters a bookshop in pursuit of a lead: this appears to be an homage to a similar scene in Howard Hawks's *The Big Sleep* (1946) featuring Humphrey Bogart as Philip Marlowe, the archetypal private investigator created by Raymond Chandler.

Karim – a former FBI agent who resigned in disillusionment after being tasked with radicalising Muslim youths in a series of undercover sting operations – is very much in Chandler's model of the fictional detective, as outlined in his 1950 essay 'The Simple Art of Murder':

> Down these mean streets a man must go who is not himself mean, who is neither tarnished nor afraid. The detective in this kind of story must be such a man. He is the hero, he is everything. He must be a complete man and a common man and yet an unusual man. He must be, to use a rather weathered phrase, a man

of honor, by instinct, by inevitability, without thought of it, and certainly without saying it. He must be the best man in his world and a good enough man for any world. (13)

In the context of *The OA* as a fiction of the multiverse, Chandler's phrase 'a good enough man for *any world*' (my italics) takes on a new resonance, particularly given the events of the second season finale which I will discuss further below and in Chapter 5. Karim's sense of 'honor' is evident not only in his decision to resign from the FBI but also in his confrontation with the technocrat, and self-styled 'Prophet of the Valley', Pierre Ruskin (Vincent Kartheiser) in the penultimate episode of the season. Disgusted by Ruskin's exploitation of teenage gamers, including Michelle, via crowdsourcing and the online puzzle game 'Q-Symphony', to 'solve' the enigma of the mysterious house on Nob Hill, and equally repulsed by Ruskin's indifference to the plight of those he has used as well as his belief that he is above the law, Karim refers to him as the equivalent of 'some cheap sweatshop foreman'. Ruskin reveals that Karim has been set up by him in collusion with Michelle's grandmother, who had approached Karim to find Michelle in the first episode of the season: Michelle is in Ruskin's home, comatose, watched over by her grandmother who had aided Ruskin's scheme out of desperation. Karim is revealed to be, like Prairie, a type of 'Chosen One', selected by the house which is 'calling' him to return and to open the 'Rose Window' in its attic which is a portal to another dimension. Karim does so in the final episode and as a result sees the dimension in which *The OA* is a TV series starring Brit Marling and Jason Isaacs. The Rose Window opens onto a soundstage with a back projection of the Golden Gate bridge and the San Francisco skyline at night. The set also has a mock-up of the cabin of Karim's boat, complete with an envelope which Karim had placed on his kitchen table earlier in the episode. With Karim's opening of the window, the series shifts into metafiction which I will discuss further below and also in Chapter 5.

Karim's glimpse of this other dimension brings to mind Paul Auster's *The New York Trilogy*, three inter-linked short novels – *City of Glass* (1985), *Ghosts* (1986), and *The Locked Room* (1986) – collected into a single volume in 1987. The first two feature private investigators, with the title of the last being a reference to a particular type of mystery story. All three novels are characterised by metafictional devices which deliver their themes of the nature of reality and identity: the detectives in *City of Glass* and *Ghosts* find their identities becoming mutable as they proceed with their investigations; the protagonist of *The Locked Room*, a blocked writer, appropriates the work of a missing author and subsequently replaces him within his family. *The New York Trilogy* appears to be modelled structurally after a similar set of three novels by Samuel Beckett: *Molloy* (1951, French; 1955, English), *Malone Dies* (1951, French; 1956, English) and *The Unnamable* (1953, French; 1958, English), generally referred to as 'The Beckett Trilogy'. The narrators of the final entry in both trilogies claim authorship of the previous two texts (and in Beckett's case, also of several of his earlier works), a form of nested narration which brings to mind the Russian dolls which feature in key scenes in both seasons of *The OA*. The dolls appear first of all in the second episode of season one, in the brothel where the infant Nina is living with her aunt after her father has been murdered and where Nancy and Abel have just agreed to adopt a boy. Nancy then goes to the bathroom where she comes across, and unpacks, the dolls, immediately before hearing another child crying, investigating the sound and coming upon the young Nina, who has been put to work by her aunt and is attempting to comfort the crying child, for whom Nancy instantly falls and decides to take instead of the boy. The dolls return in season two where they are a gift from the parallel dimension version of Nina to Hap (as explained in episode 7), who uses them to explain the concept of inter-dimensional travel, and the possession of bodies it involves, to Prairie (episode 2). The first season scene with Nancy and the dolls, which immediately precedes her first encounter with Nina/Prairie, can be understood retrospectively as foreshadowing this scene with Hap and Prairie as well as subtly introducing the notion of layered identity which becomes central to the series: Nina will always exist within and beneath Prairie in the universe of the first season just as she will when Prairie occupies her body in season two.

McHale describes *The Unnamable* as a 'grotesque parody of St. Anselm's so-called "ontological argument"' for the existence of God: God is 'that which no greater can be thought' (1987: 13). This formulation requires the existence of what McHale terms an ontological 'ceiling': both Beckett's and Auster's trilogies provoke us to think about the relationship between authorship and God; if the narrators of the final entries have written the previous two, and Beckett and Auster have written all three, then who – or what – has 'written' the authors, or, for that matter, the reader? Similarly, Karim's glimpse into the dimension where he appears to be a fictional character in a TV series calls his own identity – and autonomy – into question along with the very nature of what he knows as reality. This is demonstrated in the awe expressed by Karim as he takes in the scene before him in a compelling performance by Ben-Adir. With the opening of the Rose Window, *The OA* moves not only into metafiction but also consolidates the elements of horror present in the plot involving the house on Nob Hill which I will now discuss in detail.

Horror

In his review of season two, Taylor (2019) refers to moments when the series 'dips into the more modern "puzzle house"' genre. Although Taylor does not give examples, films of this kind include *Saw* (2004) and several of its sequels, *House of 9* (2005), *Fermat's Room* (2007) and *The Killing Room* (2009). Although all of these films can be categorised as belonging to the horror genre none of them contain supernatural elements. The supernatural is present in *The House with a Clock in its Walls* (2018), adapted from the 1973 John Bellairs Young Adult novel of the same name, which is also focused on an old, ludic house and which is brought to mind by the scenes set in the Nob Hill house, particularly when Prairie and Karim attempt to 'solve' it. The supernatural is, of course, present in *The OA* although the series is perhaps better understood as presenting a wider concept of nature than that which can be accommodated by an Enlightenment-derived worldview.

In episode five of season two Ruskin explains – via the medium of taped sessions with Hap, who is his therapist in this dimension, recalling the tapes of her younger self speaking Russian discovered by Prairie in her adoptive parents' home and continuing the series' preoccupation with media technology – that the house was built in 1910 following the earthquake of four years earlier, on the site of a natural spring sacred to the indigenous Ohlone people of the area. This trope of paranormal occurrences resulting from modern construction on an indigenous site has become something of a cliché in modern horror fiction following its use in two notable examples of the genre, the novels *The Shining* (published 1977) and *Pet*

Sematary (1983) by Stephen King which both spawned a multitude of imitators. Stanley Kubrick's 1980 film adaptation of *The Shining* bears some similarity to the Nob Hill sequences of *The OA*: like the house, The Overlook Hotel, where most of the film is set and which is revealed to have been built on a Native American burial ground, seems to be alive and capable of warping reality. Ruskin refers to the House, sarcastically, as 'haunted' in the penultimate episode of season two and it certainly recalls not only the Overlook Hotel but also the eponymous structure, also capable of warping reality, of Shirley Jackson's novel *The Haunting of Hill House* (1959), loosely adapted as another Netflix Originals series in 2018, which also belongs to the 'puzzle house' genre.

The opening lines of Jackson's novel, in which Hill House is explained to be 'not sane' because it exists 'under conditions of absolute reality' (1987: 3) are echoed in the description of Hap's inter-dimensional counterpart Dr Percy's book *Quantum Psychotic* as being concerned with the psychological damage of 'unmitigated reality'. (The notion of the psychic toll that reality can take on individuals if it is not in some way mediated is present too in the poem 'Burnt Norton' by T.S. Eliot, which contains the line 'Humankind cannot bear very much reality'. 'Burnt Norton' is part of Eliot's *Four Quartets* (1943) as is 'Little Gidding', an extract from which is written on a wall in the Nob Hill house and read by Karim.) In both Jackson's novel and *The OA*, reality can be mitigated by dreams; dreams are also sources of prophecy, which is why Ruskin monitors those of the workers he employs to have them, in an act of what Shoshana Zuboff would term, as in the title of her 2019 book on the subject, 'surveillance capitalism'. Zuboff compares surveillance capitalists, such as the figures on whom Ruskin is based, to the industrialist 'robber barons' of the American Gilded Age (c.1870-1900). Like their predecessors, Zuboff's surveillance capitalists

> stand on the frontier of a vast discontinuity in the means of production with nothing but blank territory in which to invent a new industrial capitalism free from constraints on the use of labor, the nature of working conditions, the extent of environmental destruction, the sourcing of raw materials, or even the quality of their own products. (106)

This is evident in the arrogance displayed by Ruskin in his encounter with Karim.

The OA, then, can also be read as a horror text derived from the actual conditions of what Mark Fisher termed 'capitalist realism': the sense that there is 'no alternative' to capitalism and that political and economic power is concentrated in the hands of a small, wealthy elite. For Fisher this creates 'a pervasive atmosphere, conditioning not only the production of culture but also the regulation of work and education, and acting as a kind of invisible barrier constraining thought and action' (2009:16), which is one of the 'injustices of the present' Marling talks of in her 2020 essay for the *New York Times*, in which she strives to 'imagine our evolution' out of in her use of the 'tenets of genre' in her work. As discussed in the previous chapter, Naomi Klein considers season two of *The OA* to be 'actually about another world' (2019a), one in which there is an alternative to capitalism resulting from the actions of, in Klein's phrase, 'the caring majority'. Klein coins this term in her 2017 book *No Is Not Enough*, the audio version of which is voiced by Marling, in which she calls for a rejection of 'blind support' for a 'progressive savior' in favour of collective action (256). This is recalled in Marling's desire to produce narratives of 'collective protagonism' or which 'do away with protagonism entirely' in order to generate '[s]tories with goals for human agency outside conquest and colonization' (2019). For Marling, as for Klein and also for Fisher, capitalism *is* horror which is evident in *The OA* not only in Ruskin's callous exploitation of others but also in Crestwood's depleted air, as exemplified by the abandoned house, unfinished because its owners became impoverished after the 2008 financial crisis, which Prairie transforms into the site for her empowering narrative just as *The OA*, as a Netflix production, seems intended to subvert the very ideology of 'late capitalism' which Marling identifies as responsible for the series' cancellation. Fisher writes that 'without a credible and coherent alternative to capitalism, capitalist realism will continue to rule the political-economic unconscious' (2009: 78); both Klein's 'caring majority', with its rejection of a singular messianic figure, and Marling's 'collective protagonism' can be understood as attempts to re-orientate this unconscious around the many rather than the few or the one.

It is explained by Ruskin that the Nob Hill house has a dual nature: it can be experienced as simply a place of residence, or alternatively as a puzzle. The aspect of the house one encounters seems to depend as much on the house's intentions as on those of the experiencer. As such it brings to mind Mark Z. Danielewski's 'postmodern' haunted house novel *House of Leaves* (2000) which can be read either as a traditional horror narrative or as a more interactive experience if the reader elects to participate in the various codes and cyphers within it, some of which involve rotating the book physically or reading the text using a mirror. Like *The OA*, Danielewski's novel is heavily influenced by the work of the Argentinian fantasy writer Jorge Luis Borges, as discussed in Chapter 1 and below, representing the house of the title as a type of labyrinth, a recurring motif in the work of Borges. And as with *The OA*, *House of Leaves* contains nested narration, presenting layers of authorship and elements of metafiction, including references to actual world horror authors Stephen King and Anne Rice, among several other writers, who have, it is claimed by one of the novel's narrators, viewed a film of the house which shows its impossible dimensions (it is larger inside than out).

Possession

Inter-dimensional travel in *The OA* appears to involve an *invasion* by the traveller's consciousness of their counterpart's body which results in a sublimation of the host's consciousness. This is the case with both Hap and Prairie who have taken over the bodies of Dr Percy and Nina Azarova respectively. This invasion of their counterpart's bodies recalls another horror trope, that of possession. Usually in horror fiction, possession is the result of otherworldly forces taking over a human host as in, for example, William Peter Blatty's novel *The Exorcist* (1971) and its film adaptation by William Friedkin (1973), in which a demonic entity possesses the body of a pre-pubescent girl, sublimating her consciousness to its own. However, possession by a human consciousness also occurs in reincarnation narratives such as the novels *Audrey Rose* (1975) by Frank De Felitta (filmed by Robert Wise in 1977) and *The Intruders* by Michael Marshall Smith (2007), adapted to TV as *Intruders* in 2014 and starring a pre-*Stranger Things* Millie Bobby Brown as a 9-year-old girl whose body is invaded by the consciousness of a deceased older man. *The OA* is also a reincarnation narrative – Prairie jumps dimensions at the point of death – but the difference between it and *Audrey Rose* or *The Intruders* is its multiversal context: Prairie reincarnates in the body of her inter-dimensional counterpart, Nina. Nevertheless, the element of possession is addressed in a conversation Prairie has with another inter-dimensional traveller, Elodie (Irène Jacob) who informs her, in the penultimate episode, that there is an alternative to sublimating the consciousness of the host body. Rather than dominating the host's consciousness – which she considers to be 'vicious' – Elodie 'integrates' with it, which allows her to remember the host's memories, something Prairie has struggled to do with Nina.

Elodie's use of the term 'integrate' brings to mind another recent horror TV series, *The Exorcist* (2016-18), a sequel to Friedkin's film, in which the demonic entities which possess human beings seek not to destroy them – as was the case in Friedkin's film and Blatty's source novel – but to merge with them, in order to 'pass' for their victims and carry out their plan to enslave humanity. Elodie urges Prairie to integrate with Nina, telling her that by doing so she will become 'whole'; as Prairie learns from the host of the clandestine nightclub SYZYGY Nina frequents (season two, episode four), Nina is in many ways Prairie's opposite, vivacious and sensual, with a bawdy sense of humour, whereas Prairie is rather ascetic and taciturn. This opposition recalls the classic horror text of a divided self, *The Strange Case of Dr. Jekyll and Mr Hyde* by Robert Louis Stevenson (1886) as well as a film inspired by it (although adapted directly from the novel *The Strange Case of Mr. Pelham* [1957] by Anthony Armstrong, itself influenced by Louis Stevenson's text, as its title indicates), *The Man Who Haunted Himself* (1970), in which a conservative individual generates a libertine double following an NDE. I discuss the ethics of inter-dimensional travel of the kind practiced by Hap and Prairie, and anticipated by the members of the Crestwood group, particularly Steve who sees relocating to another dimension as a solution to his many social problems, in the section on Multiversal Fiction below.

H.P. Lovecraft

While impersonating Nina at SYZYGY, in the second season's fourth episode, Prairie participates in a performance, which Nina regularly delivers, that involves her acting as a medium for an octopus with psychic abilities. The creature is known to the audience as 'Old Night' but reveals its true identity to Prairie as Azrael, the Angel of

Death from Jewish and Islamic tradition. Old Night makes reference to his 'brothers and sisters in the sea' which, along with his celaphopodic nature, brings to mind the otherworldly creatures from the works of the American horror and 'weird' fiction writer H.P. Lovecraft, particularly the cosmic deity Cthulhu, described in the short story 'The Call of Cthulhu' (1928) as having 'an octopus-like head whose face was a mass of feelers' (148); these feelers also recall the sea creature consumed by Homer on his first inter-dimensional 'jump' in the fourth episode of season one, discussed further below. Like Old Night, Cthulhu has psychic abilities: asleep for centuries deep under the ocean, Cthulhu's dreams influence civilisation, creating a general sense of anxiety and unease. Despite being an Angel of Death, Old Night seems benign in his disposition towards humans, in contrast to his siblings' view that communicating with them is a 'waste of time', recalling the indifference towards humanity displayed by Cthulu and the other 'Great Old Ones' in Lovecraft's work. Although he claims the sea to be his home, Old Night demonstrates knowledge of the true, multiversal nature of reality which suggests that he too may be a type of inter-dimensional traveller and/ or an extra-terrestrial being. Marling and Batmanglij may have been influenced here by claims made by a team of researchers in the August, 2018 edition of the scientific journal *Progress in Biophysics and Molecular Biology* (Vol. 136) that the octopus has extra-terrestrial origins, as well as by Lovecraft's fiction. Another possible source of influence might be film-makers Justin Benson and Aaron Moorhead's 2014 fusion of 'body horror' (a sub-genre characterised by a preoccupation with and representation of the human body and its violation) and romance *Spring*, in which an ancient mutant which can pass for human but regularly reverts to a cephalopodic form, reminiscent of Cthulhu, falls in love with a young American fugitive, hiding out in present-day Italy. *Spring* is also recalled in the erotic undertones of Old Night's fusing with Prairie as she becomes his medium.

Old Night offers to reveal Prairie's 'true face' to her but can only do so after he kills her for 37 seconds, creating another NDE in which Prairie finds herself on a passenger jet where she approaches a woman with short blonde hair, later revealed to be the character, Brit – apparently, a version of Marling - into whom Prairie jumps in the second season finale. This again indicates Old Night's knowledge of the multiverse, if not his ability to travel through it. Old Night appears only in a single episode and is not discussed subsequently, but nevertheless the scene involving Prairie's mediumship of him is one of the most memorable in the second season, if not necessarily for the reasons Marling and Batmanglij may have desired: for *Guardian* reviewer Jack Seale (2019) the scene was the 'last straw' for his participation in the series, which he dismissed as 'hokey bunkum' and 'handsomely mounted rubbish'.[3]

Inland Empire

As mentioned earlier, Sean Hutchinson (2017) of Inverse magazine criticised Marling and Batmanglij for crowding *The OA* with under-developed ideas as a result of the creative freedom provided by Netflix, in contrast to the focusing limitations imposed upon them with their films, particularly the low-budget *Sound of My Voice*. However, this overlooks the fact that *The OA* was initially planned to encompass five seasons and so it may have been Marling and Batmanglij's intention to develop elements such as Old Night – or the revelation in the sixth episode of season two that not only is Prairie's FBI trauma counsellor Rahim aware of her angelic status and of the existence of the multiverse, he has also been 'sent', by some unnamed entity, to help the Crestwood group reach her across dimensions – in subsequent seasons. Certainly, the elements of foreshadowing in season one indicate that Marling and Batmanglij had a clear vision in mind, at least for the first two seasons. This is evident in, for example, Homer's jump, in the first season's fourth episode, to the Treasure Island facility in which Prairie will be incarcerated in season two. To end his NDE, and return to his Home dimension, Homer follows Khatun's earlier advice to Prairie (season one, episode four) and eats a living thing, a sea creature (foreshadowing Old Night and his 'brothers and sisters in the sea') from the facility's aquarium, which is a scale model of Hap's dungeon, as French observes in the season two finale. Homer also listens to a tape of one of his NDEs – Hap having developed the ability to record audio across dimensions, another example of the importance of media technology to the series – in which another aspect of inter-dimensional travel is introduced: it is possible for a traveller to co-exist with their counterpart in the same dimension, as Homer does with Dr Roberts during this jump; later, when Roberts has a session with Prairie they hear a noise coming from the ceiling above them which Prairie explains is Homer. This brings to mind a similar scene in David Lynch's *Inland Empire* (2006), in which Laura Dern's character Nikki disturbs a film set on which an earlier version of herself is performing. *Inland Empire* is further recalled in the use of metalepsis in the season two finale of *The OA* when, as in Lynch's film, what the viewer had believed to be a fictional reality is revealed to be a soundstage (which is, of course, still a fictional reality but one which is nested, Russian Doll-like, within a larger one) on which a narrative-within-a-narrative is being filmed. Furthermore, the round Rose Window seems to be a reference to what Fisher identifies as *Inland Empire*'s 'dominant motif' of 'the hole' which he considers to be a 'threshold' (2016: 57).

New Age Genre

Writing for the website *Screenhub* (2019), Adrian Martin has suggested that the second season of *The OA* 'consolidates a growing twenty-first century genre across film and TV' which he identifies as the 'New Age Genre'. Martin traces the origins of this genre to *The Matrix* and argues that it was continued in *Sense8* which also indicated that 'the genre has gravitated more to TV than movies', citing HBO's short-lived series *Here and Now* (2018) as further evidence of its presence in that medium. As indeed is *The OA*'s second season which displays the characteristic elements of the genre, according to Martin, which include a 'group or network of "interconnected" characters' who share a psychic connection and experience of visions and who are involved in the solution of a 'vast mystery, conspiracy or riddle' for which 'there are cryptic clues scattered everywhere'. Furthermore, *The OA* also demonstrates an 'earnest socio-political sensitivity', particularly in relation to marginalised members of society, which Martin considers to be fundamental to the New Age genre. Martin makes reference to the film director – and fan of *The OA*'s first season – Jessica Redenbach's view that this focus on a group of characters is a flaw in the second season as it has the effect of 'dissolving its central focus on Prairie' whom she considers to be the series' 'emotional centre'. However, Redenbach's interpretation of the series, and Prairie's role within it, seems to be based on established generic and diegetic conventions (just as Archbold's understanding of the audience's viewing practices comes across as somewhat out of date, as discussed in Chapter 2), which does not take into consideration Marling and Batmanglij's ambitions for a narrative of 'multiple protagonism' rather than a traditional 'Chosen One' story – although elements of that tradition do exist, at least superficially, in the series, with both Prairie and Karim.

Season two can be understood, then, as an attempt to undo this established narrative trope in a similar manner to the way in which the final episode of *Buffy the Vampire Slayer*, entitled 'Chosen' (2003), replaces the unique figure of the Slayer with an army of equally powerful young women (as was subsequently explored in the comic book series). Martin recognizes *The OA* as a 'new kind of screen story, for better or for worse' – he is not impressed by the second season compared to the first – and identifies the presence of a 'chosen individual' as antithetical to the concerns of the New Age genre as such a character has the potential to become a 'messiah or guru' which 'could turn out to be really bad news for the human race' and concludes that an emphasis on a character group is the only way *The OA* can 'get its New Age message across'. (It is worth noting here that Morrison attempted a similar subversion of the 'chosen individual' narrative in *The Invisibles* by focusing on the relationships and inter-personal dynamics of the eponymous anarchist group. The group includes both a charismatic leader figure in King Mob and a messiah figure in the character of Jack Frost whose roles and status in the group are constantly questioned and re-configured as the series develops. As discussed above, *The Matrix* bears strong thematic and visual similarities to *The Invisibles*, so perhaps the emergence of the New Age genre can be traced back earlier to it.)

Multiversal Fiction

'To exist is to survive unfair choices,' the celestial entity Khatun tells Prairie in the fourth episode of season one, a remark which can be understood as a reference not only to the endurance Prairie has displayed while Hap's prisoner, but also to her status as an inter-dimensional traveller who can 'jump' to another dimension at the point of death. Prairie does so at the end of season one after she is struck by a stray bullet from a high school shooter, an event foreshadowed in the previous episode by Prairie digging a pencil lead out of her leg after a frustrated Steve attacks her, as well as in episode five when a TV news report about a shooting at mall, from which the shooter escapes, plays in the background as BBA regards herself in a mirror, and also in episode six when Prairie hears gunshots and 'a clanking sound, like silverware' during her nightmare. The shooting is the 'great evil' that Khatun tells Prairie she must work with a group of five to prevent in episode four. It has been Prairie's choice to thwart this evil but we might ask if such a choice is 'fair' given the consequences. Prairie subsequently takes over the body of her counterpart, Nina, in the 2016 of a parallel dimension which closely resembles her own world, with the exception that Joe Biden is president rather than Barack Obama. Taking over Nina's identity gives Prairie access to her considerable wealth, as represented by her luxurious apartment and expensive wardrobe, which impress Prairie; these material comforts can be seen as a reward for the hardship Prairie has endured, albeit one which is experienced only fleetingly. They are also representative of the life she could have had in her own dimension, as she acknowledges in the second season finale.

The sixth episode of the season is titled 'Forking Paths', a reference to the Borges 1941 short story 'The Garden of Forking Paths' which predates the 'relative state formulation' of physicist Hugh Everett, proposed in 1957 and later named the 'many-worlds' theory by another physicist, Bruce DeWitt. Everett posited that our universe is, in fact, part of a potentially infinite multiverse in which everything that possibly could have happened did happen, in parallel dimensions, on other worlds, which brings to mind Marling's film *Another Earth*, as discussed in Chapter 1. In Borges' story – which McHale considers to be a key text in the move from modernist to postmodernist fiction in the twentieth century due to its ontological, rather than epistemological, preoccupations and corresponding focus on 'problems of modes of being' rather than those of 'knowledge' (1987: 10) – the narrator makes reference to a labyrinthine novel which is revealed to also be a model of the multiverse. Hap makes his own map of the multiverse in season two, which he refers to as 'an actual garden of forking paths' in reference to the flowers he cultivates from the brains of NDE experiencers after they return to life. Hap's map is constructed from human beings, including the dimensional counterparts of members of the Crestwood group. Furthermore, the labyrinthine nature of the novel in Borges' story recalls the maze-like nature of the Nob Hill house in 'puzzle' mode. Although 'The Garden of

Forking Paths' is not itself a multiversal fiction, as characters do not cross dimensions, for McHale its 'possibilities' (21) were developed in the work of subsequent postmodernist writers, notably by Robert Coover in his short story collection *Pricksongs & Descants* (1969).

Its influence is evident too in the superhero comics published by DC in the genre's 'Silver Age' (c.1956-1970), particularly those edited by Julius Schwartz who introduced a science fiction sensibility to superhero narratives, including the creation of a multiverse for DC's stable of characters. Schwartz was responsible for a new iteration of the superhero character The Flash – originally created in 1940 by Gardner Fox and Harry Lampert as the 'secret identity' of college student Jay Garrick – a police scientist named Barry Allen who, in his debut appearance (in *Showcase* #4, October, 1956) is seen, prior to his acquisition of super powers, reading a comic featuring Garrick as the Flash, which brings to mind the metalepsis of *The OA*'s final episode. When Allen subsequently receives powers of super-speed similar to those of Garrick, and following a similar laboratory accident, he decides to become a superhero, modelling himself on Garrick's superhero identity as The Flash. The 1961 story 'The Flash of Two Worlds' (*The Flash* #123, September, 1961), edited by Schwartz and written by Gardner, with artwork by Carmine Infantino, unites Garrick and Allen after the latter uses his powers to travel inter-dimensionally to a world, later named 'Earth-Two', where Garrick, and the other superhero characters from DC's 'Golden Age' (c. 1938-1945) exist as 'real' people. Fox is himself a character in the story – a writer who, like many other creatives, is tuned in subconsciously to Earth-Two, drawing inspiration from it for the comics he creates in his own dimension (Fox and Schwartz were likely influenced by the psychic emanations of Lovecraft's Cthulhu here; Schwartz was Lovecraft's literary agent in the 1930s). Again, this anticipates the use of metalepsis as well as the trope of interdimensional travel present in *The OA*.

Alternative History

The concept of multiple earths is also a central tenet of David Lewis's philosophical thesis of 'modal realism' in which he argues for the existence of a 'plurality of worlds' (2011: vii); Lewis refers to this plurality as *possibilia*. For Lewis, all possible worlds exist somewhere, but are mutually isolated because '[t]here are no spatio-temporal relationships at all between things that belong to different worlds'; there is also no causal relationship between events in possible worlds (2). However, neither restriction necessarily applies in the case of multiversal fiction, including *The OA*. In the second season's penultimate episode, the inter-dimensional traveller Elodie tells Prairie, while encouraging her to integrate with Nina, that they 'share the same beginning' and that she must 'get back to the time before your paths split', another reference to Borges and also to the point of 'divergence' necessary for the creation of alternative history fiction – a sub-genre which intersects with that of multiversal fiction and to which *The OA*, with its representation of a world in which Joe Biden is the American president in 2016, belongs. Not all, or even most, alternative history fiction is multiversal, however, as the worlds presented in it tend to be, in Lewis's phrase, 'mutually isolated' (2011:2). This is the case, for example, in the work of Harry Turtledove, the 'Master of Alternative History', whose divergent worlds are discrete, with the notable exception of his Young Adult series, *Crosstime Traffic* (2003–2008), in which inter-dimensional travel is facilitated by the eponymous organisation. A similar premise is found in the 'Paratime' series created by H. Beam Piper in 1948 and subsequently developed by John F. Carr; and in the *Imperium* novels (1962–1990) of Keith Laumer. Elodie describes herself to Prairie as a 'creature of balance' bringing to mind the work of Michael Moorcock – who, as editor of the science fiction magazine *New Worlds* in the mid-1960s was instrumental in the genre's shift from 'hard' narratives, focused on technological and scientific realism, to the more experimental and literary sensibility of the 'New Wave' of science fiction which *The OA* recalls – and whose own multiversal fiction features the Eternal Champion, a figure who endlessly reincarnates across dimensions and throughout history and who seeks to strike a 'cosmic balance' between the forces of Law and Chaos. Furthermore, Elodie's description of herself to Hap in season two's fourth episode as an inter-dimensional traveller who wanders the multiverse recalls the title of a collection of three of Moorcock's multiversal novels, *A Nomad of the Time Streams* (1982).

As in Moorcock's work, the multiverse of *The OA* is characterised, as Elodie explains to Prairie, by repetition of not only events but also roles: Hap is Prairie's 'shadow', according to Elodie, and they are bound to each other, and to Homer, 'across many dimensions, like a cosmic family'. Prairie is, therefore, destined to constantly encounter both Hap and Homer. Furthermore, events in one dimension effect those in others, as is shown in a flashback to Prairie telling the group her story in the abandoned house in Crestwood which focuses on Buck, before cutting to a scene in which his dimensional counterpart, Michelle Vu, starts to play Q-Symphony, the game designed by Ruskin which will lure her to the Nob Hill house and lead to Karim's involvement with Prairie. Elodie describes this inter-dimensional resonance as an 'echo'; when Prairie asks how she can 'escape' from the echo she is currently experiencing, Elodie informs her that to do so is 'dangerous' as it risks entering another dimension in which she would forget not only her own identity but also those of Hap and Homer. Homer has already forgotten his identity after having jumped dimension at the end of season one with the rest of the dungeon captives who have retained theirs, even Rachel who has been injured in the jump, resulting in aphasia and the loss of her ability to sing. Although Homer has entered the body of his dimensional counterpart Dr Roberts, Roberts' consciousness has remained dominant. Homer only remembers his identity, and his time in Hap's dungeon with Prairie and the others, when under stress in the final episode. When subsequently asked by another former dungeon captive Renatta (Paz Vega) if he is Homer or Dr Roberts, he replies 'both', indicating that he has integrated with his host. After Prairie has allowed Nina's consciousness to reassert itself, she visits Hap who, it transpires, she had hired, after reading *Quantum Psychotic*, to uncover the true nature of the Nob Hill house. Prairie's consciousness returns to dominance after Hap shows her his 'garden', resulting in a confrontation between the two which takes them outside to the grounds of the Treasure Island facility where Hap has placed machines which will perform the movements required to travel to yet another dimension, one which Hap has glimpsed after eating a petal from a flower that has blossomed from one of the NDE experiencers in his 'garden'. This is the dimension shown in the season finale, in which Jason Isaacs and Brit Marling play versions of themselves as actors in a TV show resembling *The OA*, who are also a married couple. In this dimension, Hap tells Prairie, everyone will refer to her as 'The OA' except for Prairie herself. Furthermore, while she will not forget her previous experiences across dimensions, she will not believe them, suggesting that Prairie-as-Brit may be injured in this new dimension, potentially providing Hap with power over her. Clearly, this new dimension presents Hap with a preferable alternative to the one he currently occupies even though he admits he prefers it to the dimension of season one. This recalls Steve's motivations for insisting the tribe jump dimension as expressed in the third episode of season two, which I will now discuss in terms of social mobility.

The Multiverse and Social Mobility

In episode three of season two, trying to convince the group – particularly French, who retains his scepticism about Prairie prior to his meeting with Abel and his explanation of the provenance of the books French found in Prairie's bedroom – to jump dimensions, Steve tells them that their social problems do not exist because of any personal failings on their part but instead are a result of them existing in a 'bad dimension' where each of them has a 'crappy, pathetic life'. He acknowledges that French is a possible exception to this statement because of the opportunities created for him by his academic and athletic excellence at school, which has earned him a prestigious college scholarship, but reminds him that his younger, less achieving, brothers are not so fortunate. Steve seems to consider this reason enough for French to flee his home dimension – and in doing so, it is implied, avoid any future financial responsibility for his family – which is indicative of a lingering residue of the selfishness that had characterised his personality prior to his engagement with Prairie. For Steve, then, inter-dimensional travel comes with the potential for upwards social mobility. Prairie achieves this status by taking over Nina's body: as she tells Hap in the second season finale, 'I got to see another version of my life here, one in which I was given everything.' By this, Prairie means not only material wealth but also filial love, her father having survived into her adulthood in Nina's dimension, although he is eventually murdered there too by his enemies (just prior to the events of the season's first episode). Nina's wealth and taste are evident in her expensive wardrobe, which contrasts sharply with the cheap, functional clothes worn by Prairie in season one, and her luxurious apartment, the opulence of which overwhelms Prairie when she first visits there. In the finale, Prairie admits to having been 'jealous' of Nina, which made it easier to 'exert my will, to take what I wanted'. However, she also admits to being 'scared' of Nina; this fear seems to have been motivated by the difference in their personalities, Nina being, as noted above, a much more vivacious and sensual person – to the point of excess – than Prairie. Nina's confidence in engaging with the world can partly be explained not only by her father's supportive presence throughout her life, but also by her point of historical divergence from Prairie: unlike Prairie, Nina, as a child, did not get on the school bus which was attacked by her father's enemies and, as a result, did not experience an NDE. Prairie tells Hap that Nina 'saw this whole world, but I saw underneath it', a reference both to her imprisonment by Hap and to her astral experiences with Khatun. While this knowledge has ultimately given her power, it has also prevented Prairie from achieving upwards social mobility in her home dimension and engaging with the world to the extent that Nina has in terms of the experience of sensual pleasure and the acquisition of material wealth.

The Multiverse and Performance

In her first appearance in the second season, within a dream experienced by Karim at the beginning of the first episode, Prairie wears the same red dress belonging to Nina, which she will don to impersonate her when she visits SYZYGY. The club, and Prairie's performance there, both as Nina and with Old Night, recall the 'Club Silencio' scene in David Lynch's *Mulholland Drive* (2001) in which Rebekah Del Rio mimes to a recording of her own acapella performance of 'Llorando', a Spanish language version of the Roy Orbison ballad 'Crying', before collapsing on the stage. Steven Shaviro has described Del Rio's performance as an act of 'ostentatious fakery' (2005), while for Mark Fisher, there is 'nothing less mendacious, less dissimulatory, in cinema's history' than this scene because it draws attention to its own *artifice*: Del Rio performs a version of herself pretending to perform her own recording, in translation, of a song indelibly associated with another singer, within a film which is itself, as Fisher observes, another form of recording (2015: 16). Prairie's 'fakery' – her performance of/as Nina – is not quite so 'ostentatious', although her lack of Russian accent is remarked upon by the club's host who tells her she sounds 'American'.

She later practices Nina's accent for her return visit to SYZYGY, before subsequently allowing Nina's consciousness to become dominant, along with her true accent, so she can confront Hap. Nevertheless, Prairie is performing every bit as much as Del Rio, even before she takes the stage with Old Night, who immediately recognizes her as an imposter and knows her to be The OA. This leads Old Night to reveal his own true identity – as Azrael – to the shock of the audience. He tells Prairie he will reveal her 'true face' in her NDE, which turns out to be that of Brit, the actor into whom Prairie jumps in the season two finale. This duality parallels Prairie's own various layers of identity: her pretence at being Nina to enter the club; her occupation of Nina's body in this dimension; her status as both human and angelic being; the change in her name from Nina to Prairie following her adoption and her subsequent Americanisation. Becoming American involves Prairie's acquisition of English as her first language, and the loss of her Russian accent, with the only evidence of her earlier fluency in Russian remaining in the form of the recordings she finds in Abel and Nancy's home. These recordings foreshadow Prairie's later discovery of tapes of Ruskin's therapy sessions with Hap, which she finds in Nina's apartment. To find the tapes, Prairie has to temporarily allow Nina's memory of the combination of the locked closet in which they are kept to resurface. This brief moment of anamnesis indicates that Prairie's sublimation of her host's consciousness is not total, as will be proven when Nina makes a complete return in season two's penultimate episode, which is named after her. Prairie's performance with Old Night is cross-cut with Hap and Elodie's attendance at an opera, Handel's *Alcina* (1735), which concerns a triadic relationship between a knight, his betrothed, and the eponymous sorceress who continuously thwarts their union. While these roles might not immediately appear to map onto the triad of Prairie/Homer/Hap in terms of gender it is important to note that Bradamante, the knight's betrothed, spends a large part of the opera disguised as her own brother, the knight Riccardio: gender is therefore also *performed* within the opera which means that Prairie can be seen as the equivalent of the knight rather than Homer. The cross-cutting between the club and the theatre emphasises the importance of performance to the episode in particular and throughout the series in general, especially in season two.

Prairie's impersonation of Nina is foreshadowed by an earlier performance by Prairie, in the series' very first episode, of Steve's mother to BBA in an attempt to prevent her from expelling him from high school after he assaults another student. While they shop for the outfit – the costume – that Prairie will wear for her impersonation, Prairie discusses Steve's problems with him, telling him that he spends too much time on cultivating his 'visible you', the self he presents to the world, both in everyday life and in the YouTube videos of his gymnastic stunts. Steve responds defensively to this criticism, stating that he has a plan which involves both training celebrities and becoming one himself through starting his own YouTube channel. Performance is clearly of major importance to Steve's plans for his life. Similarly, the 'character clause' included in French's scholarship agreement requires him to behave in a respectable manner. French already does so in public, although we see him secretly take drugs – bringing to mind another model student with a secret life, Laura Palmer from Lynch's *Twin Peaks* – which he buys from Steve. Steve displays contempt for French's public persona, reminding him that he knows the truth of Steve's domestic situation, with an alcoholic mother and absent father in the 'smelly, shitty house you crawled out of' in the second episode of season one.

In her conversation with BBA, during which one of her false nails falls off, drawing attention to the artifice of her performance, Prairie uses a theatrical metaphor to describe the teacher's relationship with Steve, describing it as a 'play' with a 'cast of two' and the classroom as its 'setting'. This performance is repeated 'over many dimensions through time'. Here Prairie makes an explicit comparison between the multiverse and performance which foreshadows later events in season two, including the revelations of the finale episode. The theme of performance is emphasised further when Elodie tells Hap, in the fourth episode of season two, that in one of the dimensions she has visited her counterpart was a famous actress, a situation which left Elodie feeling 'exposed' as she was unaware of her counterpart's status before arriving there. As a result, she withdrew to the actress's flat and watched her films on DVD – in an act of binge-viewing which is comparable to the opportunities to consume media provided by digital technology in the actual world, including via streaming platforms such as Netflix. This was an experience in which she 'saw herself' in various roles which appear to be as real to Elodie as her own existence as an inter-dimensional traveller, dependent as it is on performing the role of her counterpart in each dimension she visits. As she puts it, the roles the actress played in her various films are 'all me and not me' and, as Prairie had in her first conversation with BBA, Elodie makes an explicit comparison between acting and inter-dimensional travel: both are motivated by a 'hunger' to 'understand the human condition'. Elodie tells Hap this when they meet in a bar following their initial encounter in a sauna. Their rendezvous is cross-cut with Homer's date with Yassi, facilitated by a Tinder-style app, which also contains an element of performance as each, particularly Homer, tries to impress the other.

This association of dating with performance brings to mind Erving Goffman's work of interactionist social theory, *The Presentation of Self in Everyday Life* (1956). Goffman uses the metaphor of the theatre to describe 'social encounters' between individuals, in which all are 'social actors' who take part in 'defined situations' and whose behaviour corresponds with established societal standards; spaces of interaction are comparable to theatrical stages and solitary spaces to backstage areas of preparation such as private dressing rooms. And the associations of the multiverse with drama made by Prairie and Elodie recall Peter L. Berger and Thomas Luckman's theories of the 'social construction of reality' – as presented in their 1966 text of that title – which McHale has summarised as an understanding that reality is a 'kind of collective *fiction*, constructed and sustained by the processes of socialisation, institutionalisation, and everyday social interaction, especially through the medium of language' (1987: 37-8; emphasis added).

The second season finale implies that the two dimensions previously occupied by Prairie and Hap are fictions created in a third. As Elodie earlier explained to Hap, actions in one dimension influence those in others, so perhaps the third dimension shown in the finale is the central dimension of the multiverse, from which all other dimensions spring. However, this raises questions about the source of creation of that dimension in a similar fashion to the trilogies by Beckett and Auster discussed above, which would perhaps have been addressed in the third season had the series not been cancelled. Elodie also tells Prairie that in the multiverse individuals become inextricably linked across dimensions as is the case with Prairie, Hap and Homer, if the '*story* between them is strong' (emphasis added). This echoes Prairie's earlier comparison of BBA's relationship with Steve to a two-hander play which is performed 'across many dimensions, through time' and also suggests that Elodie may be aware that she is a fictional character, foreshadowing the season finale's shift into metafiction, as had the NDE Prairie experienced while channelling Old Night. Prairie's near-encounter with Marling during the NDE – aborted when Karim kills Old Night – brings to mind the superhero Animal Man's meeting with his author, Grant Morrison, in issue 26 of the eponymous series, written by Morrison. This encounter occurs after Morrison invents a plot device to pull the superhero out of his dimension and into Morrison's own. Of course, the Morrison that does so is himself a fictional character, an avatar of the real-world author – a 'paper version of myself', as Morrison puts it (2012: 219) – as is the version of Marling Prairie nearly meets then later jumps into. The fictional Morrison explains to Animal Man that the reason the character has suffered so much recently, as depicted in the earlier issues of the series, is because that is what is required by writers to make their stories 'interesting'. The actual Morrison has stated that his reason for having his 'paper version' engage with the character was to imply that 'our lives might also be "written" to entertain or instruct an audience in a perpendicular direction we could never point to' (219), bringing to mind the trilogies of both Beckett and Auster discussed above, as well as the final episode of *The OA*.

The significant difference between the two encounters is that in *Animal Man*, Morrison (or rather his avatar) initiates their meeting whereas Prairie is pushed towards Marling by Old Night who, like Elodie, seems to be aware of his status as a fictional character. As such, Prairie recalls the characters in Luigi Pirandello's play *Six Character in Search of an Author* (1921), whose author refuses to complete their narrative, although Prairie is unaware at this stage that she even *has* an author, her use of the theatrical metaphor to describe BBA's relationship with Steve notwithstanding. Like Prairie in the season two finale, Pirandello's characters arrive on a stage set, that of a production of another Pirandello play, *Mixing It Up*, and persuade its director to stage their story so far. Sadly, the cancellation of *The OA* by Netflix means we will probably never know what Prairie's entry into Brit's body would have led to.

Throughout Morrison's run on *Animal Man*, the eponymous character begins to suspect that he is being controlled by, in Morrison's words, 'some demiurgic Gnostic overlord' (219). Here Morrison is making reference to the belief among Gnostics that the world is the creation of a demented false god – sometimes referred to as Rex Mundi (the 'King of the World') – who has trapped humanity within the prison that is reality under his rule (Morrison also used this concept in his Vertigo series *The Invisibles*, in which Rex Mundi is a character, albeit one which never actually appears on the page and which may, in fact, not exist). An obvious comparison can be made here between the demiurge and an author who controls the reality of a fictional world and, therefore, the lives of the fictional characters who comprise its population. Marling, in the actual world, is an actor as well as a writer and it is safe to assume that her counterpart in *The OA*, into whom Prairie jumps in the season two finale, has a similar dual role. Marling, therefore, not only creates Prairie's reality, she also *performs* it. This is consistent with Elodie's claim to Prairie that actions in one dimension affect other dimensions. So we may speculate that, in the cosmology of *The OA*, the performance of the fictional Brit's scripts shapes the reality of the dimension occupied by her characters, which in turn affects other dimensions. These dimensions are, of course, also the creations of the actual Marling, along with Batmanglij and the other writers on the series; but while they may also be the creation of the writers' fictional counterparts these characters might be entirely unaware of the consequences of their actions (unlike the fictional Morrison of *Animal Man*, who knows exactly what he's doing).

The Multiverse and Gnosticism

Morrison has rejected the description of his treatment of the character of Animal Man as metafictional in favour of what he terms an *anthropological* approach towards the writing of fiction. He contrasts this method with the 'missionary' approach taken by some of his contemporaries in the field of superheroes in the 1980s and '90s, the era of what Geoff Klock has termed 'revisionary' comics which attempted to inject a kind of 'gritty' realism to superhero fiction (2002). Just as religious missionaries 'attempted to impose their own values and preconceptions on cultures they considered inferior', so too, according to Morrison, did missionary writers attempt to 'elevate' the superhero genre into something more serious, which involved the 'bullying' and 'humiliation' of the characters 'native' to it. Anthropologist writers like Morrison, on the other hand, 'surrendered themselves' to the 'foreign culture' of the genre and the fictional worlds which comprise it, engaging with the characters who populate these worlds 'with respect and in the interests of mutual understanding' (2012: 218). Given the compassion for the suffering of others displayed throughout *The OA*, it is easy to imagine Marling and Batmanglij – both the actual and fictional versions – taking a similar approach to the metafictional multiverse they have created if the series had progressed.

It is also worth mentioning here that in the strain of Gnostic thought developed by the early Christian theologian Valentinus (c.100-160AD), the term *syzygy* refers to a male/female pairing, which, in terms of *The OA*, may apply to both Prairie and Homer, and Prairie and Hap. Furthermore, given that the term is also the name of the club where Prairie, as Nina, performs as a medium for Old Night, who is represented as male, her union with him might also be considered a *syzygy*. As much as Prairie might wish her relationship was purely with Homer, the two also seem to be inextricably involved with Hap, as is reflected in the choice of Handel's *Alcina* for the performance Hap attends with Elodie. In the penultimate episode of season two, Elodie describes the triad of Prairie, Hap and Homer to Prairie as a 'constellation' while they are at the bar in SYZYGY; this description resonates with the name of the club, which, in an astronomical context, is a term for three celestial bodies configured in a straight line. The double meaning of the word, in terms of relationships, is representative of the conflict between Prairie's desires and her place in the multiversal scheme of things. As part of a 'constellation' with Hap, it appears that Prairie is destined never to be rid of him.

Within Valentinianism, syzygys are the foundation of *aeons*, 'emanations' of the primal being Bythos, formed from a male and a female component. Materiality, and with it the demiurge who believes he rules the material universe, are created by the error made by Sophia, the female half of the youngest of these Aeons. Sophia's error is to 'cut herself off from her [male] consort' (Robinson, 1996: 485) and imitate Bythos's acts of creation (emanation) without him, which results in the generation of the material universe. Sophia, or rather her lower aspect, sometimes referred to as her daughter and known as Sophia Achamoth, is cast out of the heavenly realm of

Pleroma and into the material universe which she has inadvertently created. Sophia Achamoth's son is the demiurge, who falsely believes himself to be the creator of the universe. In some Gnostic traditions, the demiurge is malevolent; however, in Valentinianism, he is merely ignorant of the universe's true origins and Achamoth subtly influences him so that an element of the divine is still present in the material world. We can consider Prairie and Homer to be the two halves of a syzygy, with Hap as a demiurge who imprisons Prairie and her fellow captives in his dungeon, just as Rex Mundi imprisons humanity in the world shaped by his derangement or ignorance. Alternatively, we might consider Brit as the demiurge, in a similar manner to the 'paper-version' of Morrison from *Animal Man*; Hap, then, could be seen as the equivalent of one of the demonic entities from Gnostic thought known as Archons which prevent humanity from knowing God. Or, Prairie could be seen as the equivalent of Achamoth to Brit's Sophia. In Valentinian thought, Sophia Achamoth is redeemed and returned to Pleroma by Christ, the higher Sophia's male consort, who descends to the material plane to find her. While this may appear to suggest that Homer is analogous to Christ, it is Prairie who searches for him in the series rather than vice versa; as with the comparison to Handel's *Alcina* made above, we again see a gender role being *performed* here which is consistent with Marling's stated intentions to challenge narrative and generic conventions (2019; 2020).

Connections with Gnosticism have also been identified by contributors to the series' sub-Reddit forum, including kneeltothesun (2018) and kaaylim (2019). Because of the series' cancellation, as well as Marling and Batmanglij's silence over the plans they had for the series, any Gnostic reading of it is purely conjectural. Nevertheless, taking this approach is useful in understanding the dynamic of the Prairie/Homer/Hap triad as a cosmic drama repeating itself over time and across dimensions, as Prairie described BBA's relationship with Steve in the first episode of season one. It is useful, too, in interpreting the relationship between dimensions in the multiverse: it appears the dimension Prairie inhabits in the first season and the one she jumps to in the second are simply mirror versions of each other (bringing to mind *Another Earth*), whereas the third dimension shown in the season two finale is implied to be on a higher plane to them both as the source of their creation. However, and again with recourse to comic books, an alternative explanation may be that, as with the fictional version of Gardner Fox in 'The Flash of Two Worlds' discussed above, the character of Brit is attuned to the vibrations of other dimensions which she expresses in the fiction she authors. Rather than placing Brit in the role of author-demiurge, this explanation posits a different, non-hierarchical, relationship between characters and creator which is closer to the 'rhizomatic' arrangement – that is, a non-hierarchical one, characterised by mutual connectivity – Marling called for in fans' continued 'authoring' of the series in the statement she released following *The OA*'s cancellation (2019). Marling seems to express a desire here not only for 'collective protagonism' but also collective authorship, which dismantles the conventional notion of the author figure just as collective protagonism does away with the established model of the hero, which Marling has also opposed in an essay she wrote, post-cancellation, for *The New York Times*. In 'I Don't Want to Be the Strong Female Lead' (2020) she writes:

> I don't believe the feminine is sublime and the masculine is horrifying. I believe both are valuable, essential, powerful.

This brings to mind the Aeons from Gnostic thought, as does Marling's question: 'How do we evolve beyond the limitations that binaries like feminine/masculine present in the first place?' For Valentinians, and other Gnostics, humanity was originally androgynous and so the notion of gender binaries was ultimately something to be overcome; similarly, Marling has expressed a desire to see 'new structures and mythologies born from the choreography of [...] non-gendered bodies' (2020).

As we have seen in this chapter, *The OA* is, like *The X-Files* as categorised by Hodges (2008), a 'hybrid' text in which elements of several genres have been combined. In the next chapter, I will address how Marling and Batmanglij have also drawn upon real world events – or what Nelson would refer to as 'specific aspects of the historical world' (1997: 113) – in the construction of *The OA*'s narrative of 'critical realism'.

Chapter 4: *The OA* and the Real World

Figure 4: The Crestwood Group – Prairie's 'tribe'.

As discussed in previous chapters, *The OA* functions as an example of what Robin Nelson terms 'critical realism' in its use of elements of, as Lacey Hodges describes them, the 'marginalized genres' (2008: 231) of horror, science fiction and fantasy to create 'fictional narratives based on specific aspects of the historical world' (Nelson, 1997: 113). In this chapter I will address the most significant of these 'specific aspects' drawn upon by Marling and Batmanglij for the series, including not only two real world instances of unlawful imprisonment similar to the ordeal experienced by Prairie Johnson but also the Augmented Reality Game *The Jejune Institute* and the 'semi-documentary' about it, *The Institute*, both of which blur the boundaries between fact and fiction. In this way they anticipate, and perhaps inspire, the layering of realities presented in the final episode of *The OA*, a trope which would, presumably, have been developed further had the series not been cancelled.

Elizabeth Smart

As mentioned in Chapter 1, when Prairie leaves her adoptive parents' home in search of a Wi-Fi connection, she passes a television on which a documentary about Elizabeth Smart is being broadcast. Smart was abducted from her home in Utah's Salt Lake City on June 5th, 2002 when she was 14. Her abductors, Brian David

Mitchell and Wanda Elaine Barzee, held her captive for nine months during which time she was raped daily by Mitchell, plied with drugs and alcohol, forced to watch pornography and both starved and force-fed. After seven months in San Diego, Smart was subsequently rescued on March 12th, 2003 in Sandy, Utah, less than 20 miles from her home, after witnesses recognized Mitchell and Barzee from the true crime TV series *America's Most Wanted*. Like Prairie, Mitchell believed himself to be an angel, whose mission on earth included returning the Mormon church to righteousness, as well as a descendant of the biblical King David who was destined to fight the Antichrist. He considered himself, too, to be a prophet who received visions of the future from God. Already wed to Barzee, Mitchell also 'married' Smart immediately after her abduction, and she assumed the name Esther after the figure from the Old Testament who was the wife of the Persian king Ahasuerus. After her rescue, and the convictions of both Mitchell and Barzee, Smart became a journalist and an activist for child safety, including the AMBER Alert system which distributes notifications of missing persons across a range of networked communications media including 'new media' such as mobile phones and the Internet as well as established platforms like radio and TV.

This system is used by Buck's mother in *The OA*'s second season when he goes on a road trip with the rest of the Tribe to, first, retrieve the dresser from his bedroom – in the mirror of which Buck has seen Rachel after her death in the dimension she jumped to with Hap and the rest of his captives at the end of season one – from a thrift store, and then to consult a medium who, the group hopes, can help them use the mirror to communicate with Rachel. Buck's mother believes the Crestwood group to be a cult organized around Prairie and subsequently led by BBA after Prairie's death in the first season finale. Brian David Mitchell displayed many of the attributes typical of a cult leader in the grandiose claims he made for himself and his abilities, including his angelic status and relationship to King David, as well as his manipulation and control of both Smart and Barzee, described by journalist Charles Montaldo as Mitchell's 'doting disciple' (2019).

For Peter L. Berger, the existence of cults in the modern world is an indication of secularization and a corresponding lack of meaning in everyday life (1969). As previously discussed, all the members of Prairie's group suffer from this lack of meaning, as well as experiencing personal problems, which their milieu of the Crestwood estate in Michigan's suburbs both externalizes – with its architectural homogeneity, empty streets and sense of mutual isolation, bringing to mind the similar suburban anomie of *Sound of My Voice* – but also conceals behind the firmly closed doors which, in the very first episode, Prairie insists the group must leave open in order to 'invite' her in (anticipating the motif of doors central to the second season). We learn that her abduction further contributed to the diminution of daily life in Crestwood, particularly for its youth: as Steven tells Jaye, also in the first episode, after Prairie's disappearance the neighbourhood children were kept indoors for 'like, three years'. The abduction of children including Etan Patz (1979) and Adam Walsh (1981), both of whom were murdered by their abductors, and disappearances of Johnny Gosch (1984) and Eugene Martin (1984), who are still classified as 'missing', and the ensuing 'stranger danger' moral panic in the US had similar consequences for children in the actual world to those experienced in Crestwood, which have endured into the present day.

Elizabeth Fritzl

Marling and Batmanglij may also have found inspiration for Hap's subterranean laboratory/dungeon from the imprisonment of Elizabeth Fritzl by her father Josef for twenty-four years, between 1984 and 2008 in the Austrian town of Amstetten. Josef explained her daughter's absence to neighbours and authorities by claiming that she had joined a religious cult. Initially alone in her confinement, Elizabeth subsequently give birth to seven children by Josef who raped her repeatedly. One of the children died and three were taken from the basement to live with Josef and his wife as foster parents. The remaining three children stayed in confinement with their mother; Josef threatened to gas them if they attempted to escape, recalling Hap's use of sedative vapour to subdue his captives. When Hap first encounters Prairie, as shown in episode one of the first season, he has come from a conference where he has sold some patents; similarly, Josef supported himself by designing technical equipment and claimed to his wife that the purpose of his daily visits to the basement was to draw plans for his machines.

CONSTELLATIONS

The Jejune Institute

The Jejune Institute is the name, not of an actual organization, but rather of a fictional one within an Augmented Reality Game (ARG) of the same name designed by the artist Jeff Hull which played out in San Francisco and, to a lesser extent, Oakland in California between 2008 and 2011. ARGs are, of course, works of fiction but as both Hull's game and the semi-documentary feature film about it, *The Institute* (Spencer McCall, 2013) deliberately blur the distinction between fiction and reality, I have chosen to address them in this section rather than in the chapter devoted to comparable texts. As we will see both game and film bear a strong relationship to both seasons of *The OA* to the extent that their influence upon the series seems hard to deny, Marling and Batmanglij's lack of acknowledgement of either notwithstanding.

The game involved more than 10,000 participants, including many known as 'Inductees' who became involved following their viewing of an introductory video by the Institute's 'founder' Octavio Coleman at its San Francisco 'headquarters'. Within the world of the game, the organization is explained as having achieved wealth and influence through its patenting of a number of devices and systems including the 'Time Camera', which can produce images of the past, and The Algorithm, a formula designed to eradicate human conflict. Described as a 'scavenger hunt' by one Inductee in *The Institute*, the game also involves the search for a young woman, Evita 'Eva' Lucient, who has disappeared and subsequently become known as 'The Missing Girl of Telegraph Hill'. According to a biography on Hull's website, nonchalance.com – 'Divine Nonchalance' being the in-game term for a positive disposition towards the universe which results in a surfeit of good luck, as extolled by another organization opposed to the Institute known as the Elsewhere Public Works Agency – Eva was born in 1971 to Katherine, a 'mystic & cult member', and Blair, a 'famed financial wizard'. In *The Institute*, Blair is described by Kelvin Williams, another participant in the game interviewed for the film, as a 'scientist mysticist' [sic] and credited with the invention of The Algorithm. The bio informs us that Eva was involved in pranks and 'elaborate stunts' as a teenager which earned her 'local notoriety' – bringing to mind Steve from *The OA* – and resulted in her being arrested and expelled from high school, again recalling Steve. In the documentary, the Inductee Jason recounts how he, and two other gamers, were led to a bank of public telephone booths where they were instructed to dance to an electro track played on a boom box by a member of the 'Savants', an artistic collective to which Eva had belonged. The track ends with a sound he describes as being 'like angels singing' – bringing to mind *The OA*'s angelic imagery; the dancing also recalls the series – after which he, and the other Inductees, received a 'transcript' from another member of the Savants.

This document folds out to become a map of San Francisco, similar to those generated by French avant gardist Guy Debord and other members of the movement he co-founded, the Situationist International – which bears some similarities to the Savants; Hull's company promotes itself as a 'situational design agency' perhaps in homage to Debord – after they had navigated a city in terms of what the Situationists referred to as the 'psychogeography' of its various 'zones of feeling' (Sadler, 1999). The map produced by the Savants also includes a CD which contains a hidden track: a recording of Eva as a young girl speaking to her mother as they walk through San Francisco after school. On their journey – reconstructed in the film – they pass a cemetery which Eva explains is where 'thousands of Indians who died of Spanish diseases' are buried and a line of palm trees where Eva claims to have fed berries to 'fairies' when she was younger. The map Jason receives depicts these fairies as winged, naked humanoids which also resemble representations of angels found both in works of fine art and contemporary popular culture, including the book on angels French discovers in Prairie's room. Eva shows her mother a grid painted on a school playground which she explains is a board for 'inter-dimensional hopscotch' which 'helps you practice how to get to Elsewhere', Eva's name for a kind of interstitial space between dimensions, described later in the film by the interviewee Organeil as a 'kind of magic between'. 'Inter-dimensional hopscotch' brings to mind, of course, the movements required to travel between dimensions in *The OA* as taught by Prairie to the Crestwood group. Eva and her mother then proceed to a bookstore named Adobe Books – their 'second home' – where a guide to interdimensional hopscotch and travel to Elsewhere is shelved between two texts by Jean Paul Sartre in the philosophy section. Williams, a librarian and bibliophile, later comes across the guide in Adobe and asks the store's proprietor about it; the proprietor provides him with a box of Eva's artwork which also contains her diary written while she was a member of the Savants. Williams contacts the Savants and is drawn further into the mystery surrounding Eva's disappearance after he receives home movie footage of Eva from her high school friend, Beth. Williams finds himself increasingly appalled at the ARG game which has developed out of Eva's vanishing which he considers to be prurient and unconcerned with actually finding or even commemorating her, so decides to create an 'elegy' to her.

To do so, he locates her father's former house in West Berkeley, which abuts with San Francisco Bay. As Williams observes, the house is unusual for its area in that it has an underground basement which he breaks into one night, despite a new family having moved into the house, when he has reached a point where he 'really couldn't tell where the game ended and reality began'. Williams does so in search of an 'artifact' known as the Crystal Oscillator which will activate The Algorithm, currently in the possession of The Jejune Institute, which he has come to believe is a real organization. In the basement, Williams breaks down a door and enters a partially submerged tunnel system, the walls of which are marked with strange annotations – which resemble Prairie's scars, self-inflicted as a way of remembering the movements required for inter-dimensional travel – and where he ends up becoming lost. He is later rescued – after a lengthy period which he cannot fully recall – by a group of Inductees (Williams is identified as a 'Participant' rather than an 'Inductee' in *The Institute* because he became involved with the game without going through Jejune) who have been instructed, by the Elsewhere Public Works Agency (which has also taken over his social media accounts) to rescue him from this 'subterranean labyrinth' in an act of crowdsourcing which recalls Ruskin's use of similar tactics in *The OA*, albeit for more altruistic reasons. Williams emerges from the tunnel with the Crystal Oscillator which is recalled in *The OA* by the mirror from Buck's dresser which initiates the group's road trip; where the mirror facilitates contact with the 'other side', the Oscillator is required to activate The Algorithm which will put an end to human conflict.

By now the blurring between reality and fiction involved in both the ARG and in McCall's film should be apparent. Furthermore, *Vice* journalist Roisin Kiberd (2015) has speculated, in an article titled 'Game or Cult: The Alternative Reality of The Jejune Institute', that Hull is the creator of Cicada 3301, the model for Ruskin's game

'Q Symphony' which has also been identified as a recruitment tool for the CIA (Nicholson, 2015). It is with the introduction of Williams that *The Institute* starts, in the words of Kiberd, 'reneging its mission' as a documentary and 'turning into fiction'. This is consistent with the aims of the ARG itself which Kiberd describes as a 'living metafiction'. IMDb identifies Daniel Shoup as the actor who plays Williams (it is his only listed role) and he is in included in the end credits of *The Institute* under that name; Beth, Eva's friend with whom he made contact, is played by Chelsea London Lloyd, who has a much more extensive IMDb resume, although *The Institute* is not included in it. In total, IMDb lists eight cast members for the film, of whom four, including Lloyd, have other acting credits listed on the site. None of these four actors are acknowledged as such in the credits but instead are extended 'special thanks' (Lloyd is billed with her mother's surname of Cymrot). No actor is credited with the role of Eva and the film maintains the pretense that she is/was a real person with the dedication 'For Eva' appearing on screen just before the end credits begin. Of the thirteen interviewees listed in the credits, ten – including two of the film's producers as well as Hull, the creator of the ARG and Geordie Aitken, the training consultant with whom Hull forms a professional partnership which allows him to bring the game to an end after he feels, like Williams, it is becoming too prurient – appear under the same names in the film, suggesting they are real people rather than fictional characters as does their presence on social media (although, of course, they may be fictionalised versions of themselves *a la* the final episode of *The OA*). The presence of actors identified as such on IMDb can be explained by the presence of the 'Reconstruction Project' promoted, according to *The Institute*, in posters mounted throughout San Francisco twenty years after Eva's disappearance. The project re-enacts the 'events leading up to' this event, although the footage of Lloyd as Beth with 'Eva' is not presented as the result of this project nor, as already mentioned, is Lloyd credited as an actor in the credits, sustaining the ambiguity over what is and is not fiction.

Eva disappears at the age of 17, four years younger than Prairie is when Hap takes her, and there is speculation in *The Institute* that she too has been abducted, perhaps by Organeil, another participant in the ARG, whom she had encountered in the 1980s while attempting to access Elsewhere via the Coit Tower in San Francisco's Telegraph

Hill. This structure does actually exist and has appeared prominently in several well-known films – such as Hitchcock's *Vertigo* (1958) and Don Siegel's *Dirty Harry* starring Clint Eastwood (1971) – and TV series, including *The Man in the High Castle* (2015-19), which I identify as a comparable text to *The OA* in the following chapter. At this time, Organeil is a 'runaway' who is drawn to the Tower which he describes as a 'spiritual lightning-rod or something'. Something of an outsider artist, Organeil begins to make sculptures of animals in the tower's grounds as well as what he describes as 'little scenes' which he places in crevices in the tower's walls: the 'scenes' are 3D dioramas which bring to mind the dollhouse from Prairie's bedroom in season one of *The OA* and the various model or miniature structures in season two including the replica of the Nob Hill house, the six-sided aquarium in Dr Percy's facility – which, as French observes in the penultimate episode, is a scale replica of Hap's dungeon – and the mock-up of Karim's boat's cabin on the soundstage as well as the soundstage itself. Eva, who is also prowling the tower's grounds at this time, starts to build her own 'scenes', starting with one, which Organeil describes as being both 'beautiful' and 'spooky', consisting of flowers and a miniature tree with, as Organeil puts it, 'some strange kind of pilgrims' on a ship in the background. This recalls Hap's garden-map, constructed from the bodies of NDE experiencers, as shown in the season two finale from whose ears flowers grow, as well as the religious character Sonja's description of the Crestwood group as 'pilgrims of faith' in episode three of season two.

Organeil responds to Eva by starting a new scene which he describes as being a 'sort of room or stage' – again bringing the season two finale to mind – to which he surreptitiously observes Eva later add an image of herself, cut out from a photograph, and a light, as well as scratching the letters 'EW' (an abbreviation for Elsewhere just as OA is for Original Angel) on to one of Organeil's miniature doors. Eva then adds tiny drawings of birds which appear to be borne aloft by her light, evoking the dove that appears in the attic of the Nob Hill house in the finale of season two. These birds, according to Organeil, make him feel 'safe' in approaching Eva which leads to them developing a friendship. Eva asks him if he understands that Elsewhere is a 'way of being and playing in the world that somehow changed everything' just as her father intended to do with The Algorithm, now in the possession of The Jejune

Institute. The connection between Elsewhere and The Algorithm is made explicitly towards the end of the film by Williams who believes that, because of Eva, 'there were moments where the ordinary world was transformed' into 'something full of potential and full of mystery' which could also describe Prairie's (re)enchantment of the lives of the Crestwood group.

According to Hull in *The Institute*, who by this point we may safely assume is playing a fictionalized version of himself, he and Eva meet shortly after her encounter with Organeil and she moves into Hull's parents' garage for a month during which time she and Hull meditate together. She also introduces him to the concept of Elsewhere which he describes in the film as 'neither here nor there', calling back to an earlier remark in the film made by Organeil that most people 'have an idea of here and an idea of there': 'here is the place we are, there is the place we are not'. Elsewhere, however, is a 'kind of magical between', not unlike Khatun's astral realm in *The OA*. Organeil goes on to describe Eva as a special kind of human being with the 'right understanding' of this between-space who is able to 'take the seed within them and become a doorway to elsewhere', which is reminiscent not only of the seeds Hap extracts from the brains of NDE experiencers to cultivate his garden-map, but also of *The OA*'s dominant motif of doors in season two, as seen in the ARG game Q-Symphony as well as in physical structures, including the basement of SYZYGY from which Prairie and Karim access the Nob Hill house through the same door as is represented digitally in the game.

Organeil also states that Eva was being 'pursued' because of the transformative potential of her ability to use her 'seed'. Eva can alter reality by, according to Organeil, introducing 'unexpected novelty to situations that are frozen', which is also an accurate description of the effect Prairie has on her Crestwood neighbourhood in general and on the lives of her adoptive parents and of her group in particular. Organeil speculates that Eva's pursuers wanted to 'co-opt' her abilities for 'corporate, military or cult-like goals' at which point the camera cuts from a talking head of him to a still photograph of The Jejune Institute's founder and leader Octavio Coleman Esq. played by actor Ayre Bender (who is listed on IMDb, but only thanked in the film's credits, as Michael Ayre Bender). It is Organeil's belief that Eva has entered Elsewhere in order to become 'inaccessible' to those who are seeking to exploit her. Hull claims that, as they mediated together, Eva led him to Elsewhere which he describes as 'this entire universe, and this entire tribe', again evoking *The OA* and the trees' message to Prairie in episode five of season two, that the 'only way to recover is to form a tribe'. Hull goes on to mention theories that have arisen since Eva's disappearance that she has either been abducted – recalling Organeil's claims of her being 'pursued' – or has taken her own life, the latter of which he rejects, implying the possibility that she may indeed have been taken if she has not escaped to Elsewhere. We may even draw the conclusion that Organeil is responsible for her disappearance or perhaps even Hull himself and/or the new business partner, and close friend, he acquires towards the end of *The Jejune Institute*'s lifespan, Geordie Aitken. Aitken comes from, and recruits Hull into, the world of corporate executive training and who appears to be, like Hull, a fictionalized version of a real person who is active on social media in the real world.

With Aitken's assistance, Hull ends the ARG on a deliberately anti-climactic note which downplays the genre fiction elements present in it hitherto in order to, as Hull puts it, 'punish' players of the game who focused on those aspects rather than on the search for Eva, recalling Williams' similar disgust with the way the game had developed. The game concludes with an event at the Institute's San Francisco HQ, hosted by Aitken, which recalls Maggie's sessions with her followers in *Sound of My Voice* in which she attempts to get them to reject the 'bullshit' of modern society, although Aitken's approach is much more playful and absurdist in tone. Coleman makes an appearance, asking the gathered inductees if they still believe they have simply been playing a game, further confusing some attendees who worry that they might have inadvertently joined a cult, but also angering others who feel that they have been 'duped' by Hull and that the anti-climactic ending is the result of them having 'lost the game' (although of course this all may be part of *The Institute*'s fiction). As such, *The Jejune Institute* ARG seems to have been intended all along more as a lesson about compassion and empathy than as an adventure.

As is clear from the points of comparison made above – and indeed others, such as a sequence in which participants are blindfolded to improve their perception, just as Prairie attempts to get Steve to do by closing his eyes in the first episode of season one – there are numerous similarities between *The Jejune Institute* ARG and

The OA, so much so it seems unlikely that Marling and Batmanglij were unaware of it or of McCall's film. These similarities have been acknowledged by fans, on the subreddit dedicated to the series (Meanderthal, 2019); furthermore, journalist Lauren Anderson has compared *The OA* to the 2020 TV series *Dispatches from Elsewhere* based on *The Institute*, for which McCall is an executive producer. But this is not in any way to accuse Marling and Batmanglij of plagiarism: rather, they have taken a similar approach to *The Jejune Institute* – which, as an ARG, is an actual world event, albeit one which involved the blurring of the ontological boundary between fiction and reality, just as *The Institute* does; we might say that both are concerned with the 'reality of fiction' – just as they did to the real world cases of Smart and Fritzl. This approach to, and interest in, ontological blurring is also evident in *Sound of My Voice*, with Maggie's claims recalling those of John Titor, who declared, in 2000, on the bulletin board for the paranormal-themed radio show *Coast to Coast*, that he was a soldier who had travelled back in time from a post-apocalyptic near future in which Americans had regained a sense of community and spirituality following first a civil war then a global conflict (Sauve, 2016). It is worth noting here that one of the individuals Sauve alleges is responsible for creation of John Titor, Joseph Matheny, also co-created arguably the first ARG, *Ong's Hat* in the early 1980s; like *The OA*, *Ong's Hat* features inter-dimensional travel.

In designing *The Jejune Institute*, which he prefers he prefers to think as an 'experience' rather than a game (Kiberd, 2015), Hull also drew on 'fringe beliefs' which exist in the actual world. Such beliefs are often labelled as 'Forteana' after the American chronicler of unexplained phenomena Charles Fort, who is alluded to in the name of the radio host who opposes Coleman in *The Institute*, Commander Fourteen. These beliefs include those of individuals who claim to be the victims of 'gang-stalking', organized campaigns of intimidation, as well as the numerous conspiracies which pertain to global elites and financial institutions which have entered mainstream culture in recent years but have long been discussed in esoteric and 'fringe' culture circles, such as the scandals surrounding the billionaire Jeffrey Epstein and the cult NXIVM, both of which involved sex-trafficking. Organeil describes Hull's decision to set *The Jejune Institute* game in the 'enemy territory' of San Francisco's financial district as having 'magicalised' the area not only physically but also ideologically by bringing people from outside of that milieu together 'under joyful and hilarious circumstances'. This brings to mind Marling's education in economics and professional experience as a financial analyst (Marling, 2020) – which, as we have seen in Chapter 3, is sometimes used to cast doubt on her authenticity as an artist – and her rejection of the finance industry in favour of the production of fiction. Marling has blamed 'late capitalism' for the cancellation of *The OA*, as have some of her fans, opening up speculation as to whether her next venture with Batmanglij might be independent in nature, as they had planned for *Sound of My Voice* before it was acquired by Fox Searchlight.

In *The Institute* Hull expresses surprise that some participants in *The Jejune Institute*, such as Organeil, took it for reality whereas for him it was always an absurd fantasy. In the parlance of ARGs, the term 'rabbit-hole' is used to describe the game's point of divergence from the actual world. A rabbit-hole, also sometimes referred to as a 'trailhead', is the point of entry for players which often takes the form of a puzzle-game (just as the floor-puzzle is the entry point into the Nob Hill's labyrinthine mode for Prairie and Karim in *The OA*) or, as in the case of *The Jejune Institute*, false documents which purport to be actual texts from the world of the game. Going 'down the rabbit-hole' brings players into the fictionalized version of the actual world which is the game's setting and context. This phrase, of course, also brings to mind Lewis Carroll's novel *Alice's Adventures in Wonderland* (1865) in which the titular heroine enters a strange, absurdist dimension after following a white rabbit down its burrow. Carroll is perhaps referenced in *The OA*'s use of the term 'syzygy' which was also the name Carroll gave to of a type of word puzzle he invented (Tate, 2015).

The belief Organeil and others display in *The Jejune Institute* seems to prove Berger's observation that cults are indications of the secularization of society and a resultant, in Weber's terms, disenchantment of the world. This is borne out too by Buck's investment in Prairie's tale, and in belonging to the Crestwood group, practically from the outset in *The OA* and his unwavering loyalty, even devotion, to Prairie even after she has seemingly been exposed by French's discovery of her books towards the end of the first season. Steve too comes to demonstrate faith in Prairie although, as discussed above, this may also be motivated by his desire for social mobility (and for her romantically). Buck's own faith seems driven more by a desire for social interaction rather than mobility, perhaps particularly of a homo-social nature, with other boys. However, he also displays a longing for something other, something *more*, than the mundanity of life in Crestwood which, in its drab lifelessness, represents the depletion of American society following the 2008 financial crisis, as embodied particularly by the unfinished house in which the group congregate to listen to Prairie which recalls, as previously observed, the congregation of Maggie's followers in a suburban house in *Sound of My Voice*.

As discussed in Chapter 2, with relation to Nelson's concept of 'critical realism', Hodges (2008) identifies a stronger '"connection to the real world"' in *The X-Files* as compared to *Twin Peaks* and suggests that the latter's increasing reliance on the fantastic and a corresponding reduction in realism, particularly in its second season, was a key factor in its vertiginous decline in audience figures, particularly compared to the phenomenon that *The X-Files* would become. As the use of the elements discussed above indicates, *The OA* also possessed a strong 'real world' connection; and as already discussed the use of the Crestwood milieu, particularly in season one, established a setting representative of the diminution of lifestyle experienced by many middle-class Americans following the 2008 financial crisis. *The OA*'s success as a text of 'critical realism' lies in its combination of these, in Nelson's words, 'specific aspects of the historical world' with elements from the genres of horror, science fiction and fantasy, as discussed in Chapter 3. These real-world 'aspects' include Barack Obama's presidency of the United States in 2016, deployed in the second season of *The OA* as a point of divergence for the parallel dimension visited by Prairie and other characters in which Joe Biden is president. Their arrival there asserts the series' status as a text of *multiversal* fiction which I will discuss further in the next chapter in terms of *The OA*'s similarity to other TV dramas which engage with the concept of the multiverse and which may have served as sources of influence or inspiration for Marling and Batmanglij. Before doing so, however, I will first of all address influences upon *The OA* as acknowledged by Marling.

Chapter 5: Influences and Comparable Texts

Figure 5: Shades of Lovecraft: Prairie and 'Old Night'.

Unique as it is, *The OA* nevertheless demonstrates the influence of, and similarities to, a range of fictional narratives including works of literature and cinema as well as other TV series. In this chapter I identify several key influences upon the series, including those acknowledged by Marling, as well as discussing a number of comparable texts, particularly those which, like *The OA*, use the concept of the multiverse to construct narratives in which characters encounter other versions of themselves whose lives are either better or worse depending upon the choices they have made, fair or otherwise, in their respective realities.

Marling's Acknowledged Influences

In an interview with Alexandria Symonds for the *New York Times Style Magazine* (2016), Marling cites the 'ferocity and complexity' of the characters San, the 'wolf princess', and Lady Eboshi in Hayao Miyazaki's 1997 animated fantasy film *Princess Mononoke* as influences on the creation of Prairie: Prairie's sweatshirt emblazoned with a wolf's head can, therefore, be taken as a reference to San, while Prairie is also, like Lady Eboshi, a charismatic leader (as is San) with a troubled past. Marling goes on to cite the song 'Wood' by the singer-songwriter Rostam as a further influence for its 'dazzle' which reminded her to complement the darkness of Prairie's story with some light, as can be seen in, for example, the near-whimsical scene in the first episode in which Prairie rides on the back of Steve's bike to a shopping mall. Rostam scored *The OA* along with composer duo Saunder Jurriaans and Danny Benis, who also provided the score for the 2011 film Martha Marcy May Marlene, directed by Sean Dugan, which deals with the struggles of an abused former cult member (Elizabeth Olsen) to re-enter society and as such bears some thematic similarities to *The OA*. Marling mentions another song as being significant in her construction of Prairie: 'Queen' by Perfume Genius, the stage name of American singer Mike Hadreas, citing its 'sense of sharp-edge mystery' and the 'feeling of a character who is broken but has a certain shine because of that brokenness' which, of course, very much applies to Prairie. Another influence Marling acknowledges is the mystical novel *The Passion According to G.H.* (1964) by Brazilian author Clarice Lispector, describing both writer and text as 'mysterious' and stating that G.H. has 'her own kind of near-death experience'. The novel ends with the narrator placing a dying cockroach in her mouth, which is recalled in Homer's attempt to eat a spider to escape the dimension he has jumped to (later revealed to be the world Prairie arrives in in season two) in the fourth episode of season one.

In her 2020 essay for *The New York Times* Marling recalls discovering Octavia Butler's *Parable of the Sower* (1993), describing Butler as a 'lighthouse' for her and a role model in presenting a 'mode of resistance' to established representations of women and conventional forms of narrative. Marling makes specific reference to the 'hyperempathy' of Lauren, the seventeen-year-old central character of Butler's novel who, like Prairie, forms a 'tribe' which she does not so much lead as, in Marling's words, 'encourage', again like Prairie. Karim buys a copy of *Parable of the Sower* when he visits the bookstore in the second episode of season two. Marling finds particular inspiration in Butler's use – and also that of Ursula K. LeGuin, Toni Morrison and Margaret Atwood – of 'the tenets of genre to reveal the injustices of the present and imagine our evolution' again indicating her subversive, and revolutionary, intentions for *The OA*.

Multiversal Television

In the previous chapter while discussing *The OA* as a multiversal narrative I compared it to the work of a variety of writers in this area such as Jorge Luis Borges, Michael Moorcock and Harry Turtledove, as well as comic books published by DC during the so-called 'Silver Age' of superhero comics. I did not, however, compare *The OA* to other, similarly-themed TV series. I will now do so in attempt to place *The OA* in the wider context of the development of 'multiversal' ideas in the field of television drama and to recognize the significant contribution Marling and Batmanglij have made to this area of narrative production by building upon, intentionally or not, what has gone before.

The Twilight Zone

The season two finale – and final episode – of *The OA* brings to mind three episodes of the American anthology TV series *The Twilight Zone*: two from its original run (1959-64), and one from its third revival (2019, following earlier relaunches in 1985 and 2002).

The first of these episodes is 'A World of Difference' (1960) from *The Twilight Zone*'s first season (episode 23), written by Richard Matheson. The episode opens with an overworked businessman, Arthur Curtis (Howard Duff) in his office with his secretary, Sally (Gail Kobe), finalizing plans for an imminent holiday with his wife, Marion (Susan Dorn). This scene is described in the voice-over narration by series creator Rod Serling as a 'tableau of reality'. After finishing his conversation with Sally, Curtis attempts to make a telephone call and is surprised to find that his line is dead. A voice then shouts 'Cut!' and the camera pans to reveal that the office is actually part of a film set, bewildering Curtis. He is approached by the film's director and learns that, as far as everyone else is concerned, Arthur Curtis is the protagonist of the film they are making and that he is really George Raigan, an actor. Raigan is revealed to be an alcoholic, struggling to cope with a recent, bitter divorce and the stress of his profession. It is implied that his belief that he is actually Curtis is the result of a mental breakdown and that the vacation he is longing to take with Marion –

whose love for and support of Curtis is in sharp contrast with the disdain displayed by Raigan's ex-wife Nora (Eileen Ryan) when she arrives on-set – is a metaphor for Raigan's desire to escape the pressures of his job and the toll his alcoholism is taking on his health.

Seeking an alimony payment, Nora begrudgingly takes Curtis to the address he believes to be the home he shares with Marion but which in fact belongs to another family. She then drives him to Raigan's home which Curtis does not recognize. His agent confronts him there, informing him that production of the film has been cancelled and stating that, as a result, 'Arthur Curtis is dead'. Disturbed by this, Curtis returns to the set, which is being dismantled by stage-hands. The photographs of Marion and his daughter have been removed from Curtis's desk which unnerves him further, causing him to will them, and the world in which Curtis is 'real', to return. After this occurs, the sounds of the set being struck fade out, Marion arrives at the office, and Curtis insists they go on holiday immediately, justifying his decision to her by saying, 'I just don't want to lose you'. As they leave his office, the sounds of the stage-hands at work return and the camera closes in on a copy of the film script, which we see is entitled *The Private World of Arthur Curtis*, suggesting that Raigan's breakdown may have created a *paracosm*: an individualised projected world similar to that generated by the narrator of Beckett's *The Unnamable* as discussed in Chapter 3. The scene then cuts to footage of a passenger jet taking off, indicating that Curtis and Marion have begun their vacation and implying that Raigan may have broken down completely or even, with the closing narration's reference to an 'exit from life' by means other than death, somehow become Curtis, in the parallel dimension of The Twilight Zone.

The reference to Curtis's office and his interaction with Sally there as a 'tableau of life' in the opening narration brings to mind the sound stage from *The OA*'s final episode, titled 'Overview', as perceived by Karim through the Rose Window in the attic of the Nob Hill house. As with this set, the 'tableau' of Curtis's office includes a backdrop of a cityscape and, like the climactic scene of 'Overview', production of the nested narrative is interrupted in an act of metalepsis, as one (fictional) world intrudes on another: with the director's voice in 'A World of Difference' and by the incursion of both Prairie and the dove from the Nob Hill attic into the sound stage in 'Overview'. Karim's position gives him a 'God's-eye' view of the set, the 'overview' of the episode's title, which was foreshadowed in the previous episode by Ruskin's exchange with Karim in which he refers to the paradigm shift experienced by astronauts when they glimpsed Earth from space, which he calls a 'dazzling overview', and tells Karim that returning to the house will allow him to similarly 'gain perspective'.

Despite this apparent omniscience, Karim is awed by what he sees, the sight of the mock-up of his boat's cabin, complete with the envelope he had earlier addressed to his friend Mo, calling his autonomy into question by suggesting that he is a character rather than, not even an author, but an individual with free will. Curtis in 'A World of Difference' does have a degree of autonomy, as evidenced by his attempts to prove his existence, but experiences increasing existential terror as reality does not conform to his expectations. Like the dove which follows Prairie into the third parallel dimension, Curtis is a foreign body in Raigan's world which disrupts its reality: as is explained to Karim by one of Ruskin's research scientists, Dr. Marlowe Rhodes – whose forename can be taken as a reference to Chandler's iconic private detective Philip Marlowe, to whose lineage Karim belongs; significantly, the only character she interacts with onscreen is Karim – in the second episode of season two, 'if something from the waking world enters a dream, it is natural' but an incursion from the opposite direction is 'unnatural'.

If we accept the premise that Karim, and everyone else, in his dimension, and also in Prairie's, are characters created by the versions of Marling – and, presumably, Batmanglij too – in the dimension Karim observes from the Rose Window, then the Nob Hill house can be understood as existing on an ontological boundary between a fictional world and the actual world, which is, of course, a fictional representation of the actual world; furthermore, this representation contains a point of divergence from actual world history in that Isaacs and Marling are married within it (at least according to Hap, who seems to have quickly integrated with Isaacs and gained access to his memories). Nina seems to have already been aware of the border-status of the house, describing it as a 'portal' to Hap and telling him that the reason she hired him to help uncover its secrets is because his book *Quantum Psychotic* 'suggested an openness to liminal thinking'. As with Grant Morrison's 'anthropological' approach towards the fictional worlds of comic book superheroes (see Chapter 3), Nina seems to be interested in gaining access to another world; however, where Morrison 'enters' worlds such as the DC Universe with the god-like powers of an author – as is represented and satirized in his 'paper version's' cruel treatment of Animal Man and his family, discussed in Chapter 3 – Nina would be entering the dimension beyond the Rose Window as a fictional character, as Animal Man did when the fictional Morrison pulled him into his world. While Curtis's insistence that he is not Raigan, and that Raigan's world is not his own, can be explained as the result of a paracosm constructed due to a combination of stress and addiction, the events of *The OA* resist such psychological reductivism, particularly once the truth of Prairie's claims from the first season is confirmed at the start of the second.

'A World of Difference' appears to have been the inspiration for the second episode of *The Twilight Zone* I would like to address: 'The Blurryman' (2019), the ninth episode of the most recent revival of the series produced and hosted by Jordan Peele, best known for writing and directing the horror movies *Get Out* (2017) and *Us* (2019). In the episode, written by Alex Rubens, Sophie Gelson (Zazie Beetz) is a screenwriter on a fictionalized version of the current version of *The Twilight Zone* who is dismissive of the pulp fiction elements of the series, which she considers to be 'genre bullshit', despite having been a fan as a child, as shown in a flashback where she is enraptured by the first season episode 'Time Enough at Last' (1959). Reality begins to warp around Sophie as the narration she has written for Peele, who plays himself, changes inexplicably, indicating the episode he is presenting will, like 'The Blurryman' itself, contain elements of metafiction which it originally did not. Discomfited by this, Sophie seeks a meeting with Peele but cannot locate him on the set. As she searches for him, she finds herself pursued by the figure of the episode's title, who has also appeared, out of focus and indistinct, in the background of the episode they are currently filming as well as several earlier ones. Sophie encounters the actor Jason Priestley, also playing himself, then comes face to face with the Blurryman. He is revealed to be the series creator Rod Serling himself, rendered in CGI (he died in 1975), who has come to take Sophie to another dimension which he refers to as the 'Twilight Zone' where they 'have a lot of work to do'.

For Sophie, privileging the pulp elements of *The Twilight Zone* – the 'genre bullshit' which makes it entertaining – diminishes its social message and reduces the series to the level of being mere 'campfire stories', a term for orally-circulated ghost stories and contemporary folklore such as friend-of-a-friend tales and urban legends. The term also brings the Prairie of season one to mind: her disappearance, and return, has become the stuff of (sub)urban legend and her nightly orations to the group in the abandoned house in Crestwood have the feel of an intimate campfire gathering, the absence of a fire notwithstanding (they use candles and battery-powered torches and lanterns instead). And, of course, the campfire tale is an appropriate medium for a narrator called Prairie. Sophie fails to recognize the importance of 'genre bullshit' to the communicative power of *The Twilight Zone*, a series characterized, particularly in it is original run, by its engagement with contemporary social issues. Her flashback reminds her of the power of what Marling would call the 'tenets of genre'.

The third and final episode of *The Twilight Zone* to which I will compare *The OA* is 'Five Characters in Search of an Exit' (1961), the thirteenth episode of season four, adapted by Serling from the unpublished short story 'The Depository' by Marvin Petal. This episode – the title of which is a reference to Pirandello's *Six Characters in Search of an Author*, discussed above, as well as Jean Paul Sartre's existentialist drama *No Exit* (1944) – concerns the five characters of the title who find themselves inexplicably trapped within a large metallic cylinder, with no memory of how they got there, nor any provisions. After co-operating in unsuccessful attempts at escape, two of the characters conclude that they are, in fact, in hell (as do the characters in Sartre's play). The five – identified in Serling's opening narration as 'clown, hobo, ballet dancer, bagpiper and an army major' – are then revealed to be, in fact, toys when the scene then cuts to an exterior winter shot of a young girl picking up a doll of the major, which she places with the other four, also dolls. The cylinder is shown to be a toy barrel the girl is using to collect money for an orphanage. The episode closes with a shot of doll-versions of the characters, one of whom, the ballet dancer, reaches for the major's hand as she starts to cry.

As Hap's test subjects, his prisoners, of whom there are also five, can also be seen as his playthings and the layout of the dungeon in which they are kept recalls the stark set of 'Five Characters...' as well as *Cube*, the 1997 science fiction/puzzle-house film by Vincenzo Natali who has, according to his IMDb profile, cited 'Five

Characters...' as an influence upon it. Just as fictional characters are controlled by their authors so too are toys manipulated by their owners and prisoners by their jailers. The existential theme of 'Five Characters...' – that freedom is illusory and that individuals misrecognize their position in the universe – is comparable to that suggested in *The OA*'s final episode where Karim is exposed to the 'truth', as Nina puts it, of the construction of reality. Realising his place in the universe – revealed to him as a multiverse – Karim is, like the ballerina, moved to tears. However, it is significant that Karim is not completely overwhelmed by the experience: in the fifth episode of season two, Ruskin – via a recording of a therapy session with Hap listened to by Homer, again foregrounding the importance of media technology in *The OA* – recounts the lore of the Nob Hill house, including its origins as the site of a spring sacred to the Ohlone tribe whose shamans believed its waters gave them a 'God's eye view' of reality. This foreshadows Karim's perspective from the attic, even while it seems to reveal his status as a fictional character (or at least as the source for one, as I will suggest in my conclusion). Ruskin also tells Hap that the engineer who built the house constructed it as puzzle in order to protect the spring: the 'worthy', according to Ruskin, will 'reach the revelations on the other side of the Rose window' while the 'unworthy' will be trapped in the house and destroyed there. Ruskin's narration plays over a scene of Prairie and Karim solving the floor puzzle in the house, implying that they are the 'worthy'. Karim's worthiness – his commitment to finding Michelle Vu which confirms his status as Chandler's 'man who is not himself mean', as does his regret over his past involvement in FBI sting operations – prevents these revelations from overwhelming him completely and allows him to, as he sees it, fulfill his mission when he calls on Buck/Ian Alexander who responds to Karim's hailing of him as 'Michelle'.

Star Trek

The sixth episode of season two of *The OA*, 'Mirror, Mirror' shares its title with the fourth episode of the second season of the original series of *Star Trek* (1966-1969). First broadcast in October, 1967 the *Star Trek* episode introduced the existence of a parallel dimension, later named the 'Mirror Universe' in reference to the title of the episode and developed in subsequent series within the *Star Trek* franchise, including *Deep Space Nine* (1993-99), *Enterprise* (2001-05) and *Discovery* (2017-), the cast of which includes *The OA*'s Jason Isaacs. In the episode, a teleporter malfunction brings the crew of the starship *Enterprise* into contact with versions of themselves who embody the ruthlessness and aggression characteristic of their dimension's conquest-driven Terran Empire, an imperialist counterpart to the series' peaceful and exploration-oriented United Federation of Planets. The Mirror Universe version of the character Spock sports a goatee, whereas his Federation counterpart is clean shaven, establishing the beard as a device for indicating that a character's counterpart is an evil version of them. This technique is recalled – perhaps knowingly – but also inverted in a flashback to Hap's arrival in the Treasure Island facility after jumping dimension and entering the body of his counterpart there, Dr. Percy, who wears a full beard and also has longer hair than Hap. By the time Prairie encounters him, Hap has shaved off the beard and resumed the short, neat hairstyle of the first season. (The episode title also brings to mind *Another Earth*'s description of the planet which enters the solar system as a 'mirror Earth'.) The 'Mirror Universe' episodes of the *Star Trek* franchise present an alternative history for humanity proceeding from the point of divergence which is the establishment of the fascistic Empire rather than the benign Federation. Similarly, season two of *The OA* shows a somewhat darker version of Prairie in Nina as well as – albeit briefly – a kinder, gentler iteration of Hap in Dr. Percy.

Sliders

Where the *Star Trek* franchise presents viewers with just two co-existing dimensions, the characters in the TV series *Sliders*, created by Robert K. Weiss and Tracy Tormé and broadcast between 1995 and 2000, travel to numerous parallel Earths, each one of which presents an alternative history for humanity proceeding from such points of divergence as the Soviet Union's conquest of the United States or the non-discovery of penicillin. In one episode, which brings to mind the Biden-led America of 2016 in *The OA*'s second season, Hillary Clinton is the president of the United States in a dimension where men are the 'weaker sex', a storyline that has taken on new resonance and relevance since Donald Trump's campaign victory in 2016 and allegations of sexual harassment raised against him. Another episode is set in a version of San Francisco where the Summer of Love of 1967 continued into the 1990s in an America where Colonel Oliver North is president. Like the Clinton episode there is a certain poignancy to this installment of *Sliders* and its presentation of the city as a zone of resistance to the neoliberalism which, in the actual world, would lead to the creation of dot.com and tech billionaires like those *The OA*'s Pierre Ruskin is modelled after, whose industrial presence in San Francisco would stimulate the gentrification of the city, resulting in the homelessness crisis mentioned in the previous chapter that is, perhaps, the reason why Karim lives on a boat.

The travellers in *Sliders* are unable to choose their destinations, bringing the title of Moorcock's *A Nomad of the Time Streams* to mind, as *The OA*'s Elodea also does. Another similarity between the two series is the use of metalepsis in the final episodes of each: both episodes present a series-within-a-series which is based on the events of the previous episodes. In the finale to *Sliders*, the travellers arrive in a dimension where they are greeted by a horde of adoring fans. It transpires that, in this world, they are the subject of a wildly popular TV series, also called *Sliders*, which is based on their 'true' adventures, as depicted in previous episodes of the actual-world series. Counterparts of most of the team exist in this world – where they are called 'duplicates' – and earn a comfortable living by making guest appearances as the travellers' doppelgängers; one of them even plays the 'Slider' she is the counterpart of in the series-within-a-series. It is revealed that a psychic, known as The Seer, has had visions of the Sliders' adventures across the multiverse, which he has made into 'popular lore' that has, in turn, provided the basis for the TV series as well as an emerging new religion he calls 'Slide ology', a cult with strong resemblances to the Church of Scientology. The Seer predicts that the Sliders will die if they jump to another dimension; however, it also appears that his daughter, who is in charge of his business affairs including producing the TV show, wants to keep the travellers in her dimension so she can exploit them for the development of Slide ology which, for her, is purely a commercial enterprise. Like 'A World of Difference', 'The Seer' can be interpreted as a satire of the entertainment industry but like 'Five Characters...' it also engages with existentialist themes pertaining to free-will and determinism. Made in an era before the high production values of current 'prestige' television, *Sliders* looks rather cheap and confined compared to the cinematic expansiveness of *The OA* but nevertheless it is a series characterized, like Marling and Batmanglij's work, by an abundance of ideas. Like *The OA*, *Sliders* ends on a cliff-hanger: despite the psychic's prediction one of them does jump dimension again, leaving the others, and the viewer, to ponder his fate. Similarly, it is unknown whether Prairie has survived her jump into the body of Marling who has fallen from a great height on the set of her version of *The OA* in the second season finale.

Fringe

In the Fox television series *Fringe* (2008-13), FBI agent Olivia Dunham (Anna Torn) has acquired a range of psychic abilities as a result of her participation as a child in trials for a drug named Cortexiphan, designed to prevent the deterioration with age of the human brain's higher functions. Cortexiphan is the creation of an obsessive scientist, Dr. William Bell (Leonard Nimoy), whose driven nature and exploitation of his unwilling subjects is recalled in *The OA*'s Hap. An unexpected consequence of Olivia's exposure to the drug is her ability to glimpse, then later travel to, a parallel dimension, a skill Bell has also acquired, again bringing Hap to mind with Olivia recalling Prairie. A state of conflict initially exists between the two dimensions; this is later resolved, leading to co-operation between them and an exchange of personnel, including Olivia's counterpart. In the first season finale, Olivia is shown in the parallel dimension reading a newspaper with a headline pertaining to Barack Obama's preparations for moving into the 'new' White House; then, in the episode's final shot, the camera pulls back to show the Twin Towers of the World Trade Center intact and still standing, implying that the events of 9/11 did not take place in the same way there and suggesting that the White House was destroyed during them instead. It is later revealed that attacks did occur on that date, but destruction of the Twin Towers was thwarted by members of the specialist 'Fringe' division of the FBI to which both Olivia and her dimensional counterpart belong.

The Man in the High Castle

Loosely adapted from Philip K Dick's 1962 alternative history novel of the same name, *The Man in the High Castle* was a television series produced by Amazon Studios which aired via Amazon between 2015 and 2019, lasting four seasons. Like *The OA* it was a streaming series, hosted by the platform which produced it with whole seasons uploaded in their entirety at once. And, like *The OA*, it has not at the time of writing been transferred to any other media.

The premise of the series, and its point of divergence from actual history, is that the Axis powers were victorious in World War II and have subsequently occupied the United States, dividing up its territory between them. Footage of a world in which the Allies won the war instead – the world, of course, of the viewer – circulates via underground networks, inspiring resistance to the occupation. This footage is the product of the enigmatic figure of the series' title. The films he makes are subsequently revealed to be glimpses into a parallel dimension which is itself only one part of a multiverse. Certain individuals, such as the first season's main protagonist Juliana Crain (Alexa Davalos), are able to 'transport' between worlds. Once the existence of the multiverse is discovered by the Nazis they immediately embark on plans to conquer it, bringing Hap's own desires to mind, although, of course, on a much grander scale. Like Hap, the Nazi scientist Josef Mengele (John Hans Tester) – one of several fictionalised versions of actual historical figures in the series – has made a map of the multiverse along with a massive machine to facilitate inter-dimensional travel named the Nebenwelt, which translates from German as 'side world', recalling Hap's own mechanical devices as revealed in the second season finale of *The OA*, although again on a much larger scale. Nevertheless, Hap is himself fascistic, seeking to dominate everything and everyone around him: as Prairie tells him in the final episode, all he has is 'violence and terror and loneliness'.

As is evident, then, *The Man in the High Castle* has strong similarities with *The OA* in terms of both form and content; as with *The OA*, the Amazon series has a prominent theme of belief, as particularly represented in the character of Nobusuke Tagomi (Cary-Hiroyuki Tagawa), the Japanese Trade Minister who struggles to reconcile the policies of Imperial Japan with his own personal morality and spirituality. The series ends with the Nazi regime defeated by the resistance movement and thousands of people from other worlds pouring through the portal created by the Nebenwelt who appear to be counterparts of those who have died during the Axis occupation in a multiversal influx which rewrites history and undoes the crimes of the occupying forces.[4]

My aim in this chapter, as with my earlier discussion of genre, has not been in any way to diminish the uniqueness of *The OA*; all texts, after all, are intertextual to a greater or lesser degree. Rather, my intention here has been to situate the series in the context of Marling and Batmanglij's own *auteurism*, developing on the discussion presented in Chapter 1, by drawing attention to sources of inspiration and influence. Furthermore, by identifying comparable texts to *The OA*, I have attempted to place the series in the wider context of the development of ideas pertaining to the multiverse in the field of television drama, to which Marling and Batmanglij have made a significant contribution.

Conclusion

Following Netflix's decision to discontinue *The OA* speculation arose that a film might be produced instead to provide narrative closure for fans in a manner similar to the feature-length final episode of *Sense8* – produced as a kind of epilogue to appease fans after the second season had already been uploaded, and which had a running time of over two and a half hours. The final episode of *The OA*, by contrast, was the second shortest of the second season at 43 minutes (the longest being episode two's 70 minutes with the premiere episode of the first season the longest of the series overall at 71 minutes). However, an article by Kate Aurthur posted on *Variety*'s website five days after the cancellation announcement entitled 'There Will Be No Wrap-Up Movie for *The OA*' (2019) put paid to that possibility. Aurthur referred to a 'source close to the discussions' between Netflix and Marling and Batmanglij who claimed that their feeling was a 'two-hour conclusion wouldn't have been sufficient' for a series intended to run over five seasons. Furthermore, the source claimed that the cast had been 'released from their contracts' by Netflix and that, as Netflix produced *The OA*, there was no hope of it being continued by another network as, for example, had been the case with the sit-com *One Day at a Time*, a Sony production cancelled by Netflix in 2019 after three seasons (2017-2019) and continued subsequently on the pay television channel Pop TV from March 2020. One commenter responding to the article, Peter, raised the possibility of a graphic novel based on *The OA* while others strongly criticised Aurthur for using an unnamed, and possibly fabricated, source as well as misrepresenting Marling's post-cancellation statement as a call for 'rabid #SaveTheOA fans' to end their protest and 'lay down their swords'. Aurthur's condescending characterisation of the protesting fans as 'rabid' notwithstanding, she is nevertheless accurate in her interpretation of Marling's statement as a call for fans to 'author' the series independently of established media platforms and to integrate the themes and concerns of *The OA* into their everyday lives. Another commenter, Tony, states 'Netflix are the networks now', echoing Marling's disappointment that the platform seemed to conform to established industry practices of 'consolidation' in cancelling the series.

This call has been taken up by writers of fan fiction, such as Kate_Monster's 'Trust

Falls' (2020) which fills in gaps for season two, and the impressively thorough treatment for a third season attributed to 'zulawski' (2020), which develops the metafictional elements of the season two finale to include the series' cancellation, and fan protests against it, in its narrative. zulawaki's treatment also draws on other actual world events such as the #MeToo movement and the mutual accusations of domestic abuse by Johnny Depp and Amber Heard following their divorce in a manner similar to Marling and Batmanglij's own treatment of historic and current events as source material, as discussed in Chapter 4. 2020 also saw the release of the highly accomplished eight-part YouTube series *Invisible River* (2020) produced by Fleeting Films in, as its opening credits acknowledges, 'association with the #SaveTheOA Movement', a social media campaign to rescue the series from cancellation. The campaign's organisers also organised *OA*-themed 'scavenger hunt' events – bringing the *Jejune Institute* ARG to mind – promoted on social media with the hashtag FindTheOA. These events coincided with the worldwide 'lockdown' in response to the Covid-19 pandemic of 2020, which prohibited public gatherings and promoted 'social distancing' and 'self-isolation', and were designed to be undertaken via Twitter. Participants were asked to upload images of themselves performing the movements from the series in front of specified 'items' – water, birds, trees, purple, mustard, wolf – using the #FindTheOA tag. The movements were also used in a 'virtual flashmob' organised by Nicole Becktel of #SaveTheOA, conducted via the Zoom video conferencing medium and streamed live on YouTube on March 26th, 2020, as well as in other similar, fan-organised online events.

As well as narratives and events, fans have also produced artworks, clothing and jewellery themed after *The OA*, some of which can be purchased via the website savetheoa.com. This site also promotes a fan-designed kite modelled after Old Night – and called, of course, Old Kite – which is designed to promote the #SaveTheOA cause as part of a road trip across the US intended to 'not only unite fans in real life but spread awareness of the movement and the show to the public'. Old Kite is indicative of a desire both to continue the 'authoring' of *The OA* and to have its authoring continued by the original creative team. The authoring involving Old Kite is also representative of the attempt to erase the ontological boundary between fiction and reality undertaken by some fans of *The OA* as exemplified in the Reddit thread started after the series was cancelled, 'The OA is real and we are her tribe!' started by a user named 'u/poetic adventures' and which links to a calendar of events opposing the cancellation. The first post in the thread contains an image of the trees from the fifth episode of season two who tell Prairie 'the only way to recover is to form a tribe', a line of dialogue quoted frequently by fans to refer to their own community activities which, as discussed above, often involve the performance of the movements from the series. Such a performance can also be considered as not only another form of 'quotation' from the series but also as an act of metalepsis in which an element of a fictional world is imported into the 'collective fiction', as McHale puts it, which is, in Berger and Luckman's terms, socially constructed reality. By doing so, fans use *The OA* to relativise the actual world, under what Mark Fisher termed 'capitalist realism' with its emphasis on the individual, to promote, instead, a collectivism comparable both to the 'tribes' Prairie forms – with the captives in Hap's dungeon and the Crestwood group – in the series as well as the socialist politics advocated by both Marling and Naomi Klein. By moving into a dimension which appears to be the actual world of the viewer in the season two finale, the series seemed to be heading in a direction in which this critical relativism would become a prominent feature of its narrative. Ian Alexander has speculated that the third dimension into which Prairie, Hap and Steve jump in the finale – and to which, in his interpretation, Michelle Vu has already arrived, entering the body of her counterpart there, a version of Alexander himself, but forgetting who she is in the process until her hailing by Karim causes her to remember – is simply another dimension in the multiverse (Renfro, 2019). If this is the case – and we will probably now never know – it can be understood as having a rhizomatic relationship to the other dimensions rather than a hierarchical one as the source of their authorship. Instead we can think of this third dimension as being similar to that which contains 'Earth One' as represented in 'The Flash of Two Worlds', as discussed in Chapter 3: rather than projecting the other dimensions in the multiverse, as the narrators in the final entries of the trilogies by Beckett and Auster claim to have projected the worlds of the previous two (as also discussed in Chapter 3), the producers of the version of *The OA* in the third dimension instead create their fiction in response to those dimensions' own projections, as is the case with Gardner Fox in 'The Flash of Two Worlds' who is attuned to the 'vibrations' of Earth One's parallel dimension, 'Earth Two'.

In her post-cancellation statement, Brit Marling praised fans of *The OA* for breaking the established 'mode of storytelling', centred around a singular hero and an equally exceptional author figure, to create, instead, a 'rhizomatic' relationship between reader and text, the actual and the fictional, and producer and consumer which is 'constantly redefining the collective aim as it grows'. For Marling, the 'show doesn't need to continue' for the 'feeling' created by such a relationship to endure. Zal Batmanglij has expressed similar views about shifting the focus of fiction from the exceptional individual to multiple protagonism as in, for example, the clip of a Q&A included in the first episode of *Invisible River*. Writing for *Observer* in 2019, R. Kurt Osenlund suggests that 'while our world surely needs all of *The OA*'s earnest gifts, perhaps it's not equipped to handle them'. Maybe so; however, the point, for Marling, and Batmanglij, and for the 'tribe' that has formed out of their fans, is to change the world. For the better.

Notes

1. A role she has fulfilled several times, including for the April 2013 issue of *W* magazine, *Violet*'s May 2014 edition, and the Spring 2017 issue of *Interview*.
2. *Stranger Things* has already migrated to comic books, published by Dark Horse which specialises in licenced intellectual property, including releasing *Buffy* comics from 1998 to 2018. The first four issue *Stranger Things* mini-series (2016) is set during season one of the TV series; the second series (2019-20), also four issues, is a prequel to the first season; the short story 'Games Master' (2019), included in the publisher's anthology produced for Free Comic Book Day 2019 is set between the first and second seasons, as is the 2020 graphic novel *Stranger Things: Zombie Boys*. It is also worth noting here that the season two episode 'The Lost Sister' (2017) includes a scene with several references to *The Invisibles* are present in the form of graffiti in a street gang's hideout.
3. It is noteworthy that reviews of Marling and Batmanglij's collaborations often focus on Marling alone: the strapline for Seale's *Guardian* piece on *The OA*, for example, makes explicit reference to 'Brit Marling's mystery serial', while Amy Nicholson's online review of *The East* for Denver-based independent magazine *Westworld* (2013) mentions only Marling in its heading and is focused almost entirely upon her as a person, rather than on the film. Nicholson mentions Batmanglij only twice in her piece and only once in reference to his directorial skills; in the other she describes him as part of Marling's 'tribe' – unintentionally anticipating *The OA* – along with Mike Cahill, director of *Another Earth*. Nicholson refers to Marling condescendingly as a 'a lovely thing who would rather write about conspiracies than romantic comedies'; an 'ingénue with a Georgetown degree in economics'; and 'a Socratic starlet who excels at asking questions' and whose 'bleeding cynicism is mistaken for depth'. Perhaps this is to be expected as Marling is a performer as well as a creator but one cannot help but detect notes of both misogyny and class envy in the criticisms of Marling, particularly in Nicholson's piece: what, exactly, is the relevancy of Marling's economics degree from Georgetown to Nicholson's argument? There is a suggestion of *inauthenticity* here which parallels Marling and Batmanglij's own thematic preoccupation with deception and the construction and manipulation of reality as found not only in *The OA* but also in *Sound of My Voice* and *The East*.
4. It is also worth noting here that Jason Isaacs starred in, and served as executive producer for, the short-lived TV series *Awake* which ran for a single season on NBC in 2012. In the series, Isaacs played a police officer who, after a serious car crash, finds himself capable of travelling to a parallel earth when he is asleep. He uses clues from this parallel earth to solve crimes in his own dimension and vice versa; however, it is never made explicitly clear whether or not the parallel dimension is actually part of a multiverse or simply a dream reality.

Works Cited

Anderson, L. (2020) 'What is AMC's *Dispatches From Elsewhere* About?' [online] *Cheat Sheet*. Available at https://www.cheatsheet.com/entertainment/what-is-dispatches-from-elsewhere-about-amc.html/ [Accessed 3 March 2020]

Archbold, P. (2019) 'The Real Reason Netflix cancelled *The OA*' [online] *Looper*. Available at https://www.looper.com/161360/the-real-reason-netflix-canceled-the-oa/?utm_campaign=clip [Accessed 26 April 2020]

Armstrong, A. (1957) *The Strange Case of Mr. Pelham*. London: Methuen & Co.

Audrey Rose (1977) [film] Directed by Robert Wise. US: United Artists.

Aurthur, K. (2019) 'There Will Be No Wrap-Up Movie for *The OA*' [online] *Variety*. Available at https://variety.com/2019/tv/news/oa-movie-netflix-brit-marling-1203317355/ [Accessed 26 May 2020]

Auster, Paul (1987) *The New York Trilogy*. London: Faber & Faber.

Awake (2012) [TV series] US: NBC.

Barthes, R. (1973) *The Pleasure of the Text*. New York: Hill & Wang.

Beckett, S. (2009) *Three Novels: Malloy, Malone Dies, The Unnamable*. New York: Grove Press.

Bell, J. (2019) 'Keep Them Watching.' In *Sight & Sound*, April, 2019.

Berger, P. L. (1969) *A Rumour of Angels: Modern Society and the Rediscovery of the Supernatural*. New York: Doubleday.

Berger, P.L. & Luckman, T. (1966) *The Social Construction of Reality: A Treatise in the Sociology of Knowledge*. New York: Anchor Books.

Beyond the Black Rainbow (2010) [film] Directed by Panos Cosmatos. Canada: Chromewood Productions.

The Big Sleep (1946) [film] Directed by Howard Hawks. US: Warner Bros.

Birnbaum, D. (2016) '*The OA*'s Creators Explain Netflix's Mysterious New Drama' [online] *Variety*. Available at https://variety.com/2016/tv/news/the-oa-producers-netflix-brit-marling-zal-batmanglij-1201942744/ [Accessed 23 January 2020]

Biskind, P. (1998) *Easy Riders, Raging Bulls: How the Sex-Drugs and Rock 'N Roll Generation Saved Hollywood*. London: Simon & Schuster.

Blatty, W.P. (1971) *The Exorcist*. New York: Harper & Row.

Borges, J.L. (1941) 'The Garden of Forking Paths' in *Fictions* (2000). London: Penguin.

Broe, D. (2019) *Birth of the Binge: Serial TV and the End of Leisure*. Detroit, MI: Wayne State University Press.

Carlton, Jim (2019) 'Housing in San Francisco Is So Expensive Some People Live on Boats' [online] *Wall Street Journal*. Available at https://www.wsj.com/articles/housing-in-san-francisco-is-so-expensive-some-people-live-on-boats-11557999002 [Accessed 24 March 2020]

Catfish (2010) [film] Directed by Henry Joost; Ariel Schulman. US: Universal Pictures.

Chang, K. (2012) Q&A with Zal Batmanglij [online] *Anthem*. Available at http://anthemmagazine.com/qa-with-zal-batmanglij/ [Accessed 24 February 2020]

Counterpart (2017-2019) [TV series] Created by Justin Marks. US: Starz.

Danielewski, M. (2000) *House of Leaves*. New York: Pantheon Books.

Deburge, P. (2016) 'Why *The OA* is one of the year's most important films' [online] *Variety*. Available at https://variety.com/2016/tv/columns/the-oa-netflix-brit-marling-film-critic-appreciation-1201948242/ [Accessed 23 January 2020]

De Felitta, F. (1975) *Audrey Rose*. New York: Putnam.

Dick, P. K. (1962) *The Man in the High Castle*. New York: Putnam.

-(1974) *Flow My Tears, the Policeman Said*. New York: Doubleday.

-(1981) *VALIS*. New York: Bantam.

-(1981) *The Divine Invasion*. New York: Timescape Books.

Dispatches from Elsewhere (2020-) [TV series] Created by Jason Segal. US: AMC.

Durkheim, E. (2013 [1893]) *The Division of Labour in Society*. New York: Simon & Schuster.

Ellis, W. et al (2002-2004) *Global Frequency*. New York: DC Comics.

The Endless (2017) [film] Directed by Justin Benson; Aaron Moorhead. US: Well Go USA Entertainment.

The Exorcist (1973) [film] Directed by William Friedkin. US: Warner Bros. Pictures.

The Exorcist (2016-2017) [TV series] Created by Jeremy Slater. US: Fox.

Feuer, Jane; Kerr, Paul; Vahimagi, Tise (eds) (1984) *MTM: Quality Television*. London: BFI.

Fisher, M. (2009) *Capitalist Realism: Is There No Alternative?* Winchester, UK: Zero Books.

-(2016) *The Weird and The Eerie*. London: Repeater Books.

Fringe (2008-2013) [TV series] Created by J.J. Abrams; Alex Kurtzman; Robert Orci. US: Fox.

French, A. (2017) 'Naomi Klein and Brit Marling talk Trump, branding, protest and activism' [online] *Los Angeles Times*. Available at https://www.latimes.com/books/la-et-jc-naomi-klein-20170623-story.html Accessed 14 February 2020.

Goffman, E. (1956) *The Presentation of Self in Everyday Life*. New York: Doubleday.

Gray, C. (2014) *Leaving the 20th Century: The Incomplete Work of the Situationist International*. Bread and Circuses Publishing.

Heffernan, V. (2016) *Magic and Loss: The Internet as Art*. New York: Simon & Schuster.

Hutchinson, S. (2017) '*Sound of My Voice* proves *The OA* wasn't meant for Netflix' [online] Inverse. Available at https://www.inverse.com/article/25997-the-oa-season-2-sound-of-my-voice-prairie-original-angel-maggie [Accessed 31 January 2020]

IMDb (Nd.) Biography: Vincenzo Natali [online] IMDb. Available at https://www.imdb.com/name/nm0622112/bio [Accessed 18 May 2020]

Inland Empire (2006) [film] Directed by David Lynch. US/France: Studio Canal.

The Institute (2013) [film] Directed by Spencer McCall. US: Argot Pictures.

Intruders (2014) [TV series] Created by Glen Morgan. UK: BBC Worldwide.

Jackson, S. (1987) *The Haunting of Hill House*. London: Robinson Publishing.

Kaaylim (2019) 'Theory: *The OA* is a modern version of the "Hymn of the Pearl", an ancient gnostic poem' [online] *Reddit*. Available at https://www.reddit.com/r/TheOA/comments/9jg8bo/theory_the_oa_is_a_modern_version_of_the_hymn_of/ [Accessed 28 April 2020]

Kate_Monster (2020) *Trust Falls* [online] Available at https://archiveofourown.org/works/20930669/chapters/49760069 [Accessed 26 May 2020]

Kiberd, R. (2015) 'Game or Cult: The Alternative Reality of The Jejune Institute' [online] *Vice*. Available at https://www.vice.com/en_us/article/jp54ky/game-or-cult-the-alternate-reality-of-the-jejune-institute) [Accessed 31 January 2020]

Klein, N. (1999) *No Logo: Taking Aim at the Brand Bullies*. London: Picador.

- (2017) *No is Not Enough: Resisting Trump's Shock Politics and Winning the World We Need*. London: Penguin.

- (2019a) [online] Twitter. Available at https://twitter.com/naomiaklein/status/1114161355974746113?lang=en [Accessed 24 March 2020]

- (2019b) [online] Twitter. Available at: https://twitter.com/naomiaklein/status/1165087456313712640?lang=en [Accessed 24 March 2020]

Klock, G. (2002) *How to Read Superhero Comics and Why*. New York: Continuum.

Kneeltothesun (2018) '*The OA* = Ennoia (The Gnostic Original Angel)' [online] *Reddit*. Available at https://www.reddit.com/r/TheOA/comments/7w8p14/the_oaennoia_the_gnostic_original_angel/ [Accessed 28 April 2020]

Hill Street Blues (1981-1987) [TV series] Created by Steve Bochco, Michael Kozzoll. US: MTM Productions.

Hodges, Lacey (2008), in *The Essential Science Fiction Television Reader* (2008), J.P. Telote (ed.). Lexington, KY: University Press of Kentucky.

The House with a Clock in its Walls (2018) [film] Directed by Eli Roth. US: Universal Pictures.

The Leftovers (2014-2017) [TV series] Created by Damon Lindelof and Tom Perrotta. US: HBO.

Lewis, D. (1986) *On the Plurality of Worlds*. Oxford, UK: Blackwell Publishing Ltd.

Lilyhammer (2012-2014) [TV series] Created by Anne Bjørnstad; Eilif Skodvin. Norway/US: NRK1/Netflix.

Lost (2004-2010) [TV series] Created by Jeffrey Lieber, J.J. Abrams, Damon Lindelof. US: ABC.

Lou Grant (1977-1982) [TV series] Created by James L. Brook, Allan Burns, Gene Reynolds. US: MTM Productions.

Lovecraft, H.P. (1928) 'The Call of Cthulhu' in *The Call of Cthulhu and Other Weird Stories* (1999). London: Penguin Books.

McHale, B. (1987) *Postmodernist Fiction*. London: Methuen.

The Man in the High Castle (2015-2019) [TV series] Created by Frank Spotniz. US: Amazon Studios.

The Man Who Haunted Himself (1970) [film] Directed by Basil Dearden. UK: Warner-Pathé.

Marling, B. (2019) [online] Twitter. Available at https://twitter.com/britmarling/status/1165013288532332544?s=20 [Accessed 24 Feb 2020]

-(2020) 'I Don't Want to Be the Strong Female Lead' [online] *New York Times*. Available at https://www.nytimes.com/2020/02/07/opinion/sunday/brit-marling-women-movies.html [Accessed 24 February 2020]

Marshall, M. (2007) *The Intruders*. London: HarperCollins.

Martin, A. (2019) The OA Part II: Dawn of the New Age Genre? [online] *Screenhub*. Available at https://www.screenhub.com.au/news-article/news/television/adrian-martin/the-oa-part-ii-dawn-of-the-new-age-genre-257623 [Accessed 25 May 2020]

The Matrix (1999) [film] Directed by The Wachowskis. US: Warner Bros. Pictures.

Meanderthal, (2019) 'The Institute (2013) - "A documentary on the Jejune Institute, a mind-bending San Francisco phenomenon (ARG) where 10,000 people became "inducted" without ever quite realizing what they'd signed up for." Deals with interdimensional travel and likely a big inspiration for The OA. (Spoilers?)' [online] *Reddit*. Available at: https://www.reddit.com/r/TheOA/comments/b5iegt/the_institute_2013_a_documentary_on_the_jejune/?utm_source=share&utm_medium=ios_app [Accessed 26 February 2020]

Mittell, J. (2006) 'Narrative Complexity in Contemporary American Television' in *The Velvet Light Trap No. 58*, Fall 2006. Austin, TX: University of Texas Press.

Montaldo, C. (2019) Profile of Elizabeth Smart Kidnapper Brian David Mitchell [online] *Thought. co.* Available at https://www.thoughtco.com/profile-of-elizabeth-smarts-kidnapper-brian-mitchell-971140 [Accessed 24 February 2020]

Moorcock. M. (1982) *A Nomad of the Time Streams.* New York: Bookspan.

Morrison, G. (2012) *Supergods: Our World in the Age of the Superhero.* London: Vintage.

Morrison, G.; Truog, C.; Farmer, M.; et al (1990) *Animal Man* #26. New York: DC Comics.

Morrison, G.; Jimenez, P.; Stokes, J.; et al (1997) *The Invisibles* Vol. 2, #5. New York: Vertigo/DC Comics.

Mulholland Drive (2001) [film] Directed by David Lynch. US: Universal Pictures.

Nabokov, V. (1962) *Pale Fire.* New York: Putnam.

Nelson, Robin (1997) *TV Drama in Transition: Forms, Values and Cultural Change.* London: Macmillan.

Nicholson, A. (2013) 'In *The East* Brit Marling takes on hipster hobos with humor' [online] *Westword.* Available at https://www.westword.com/film/in-the-east-brit-marling-takes-on-hipster-hobos-with-humor-5120886 [Accessed 13 February 2020]

Nicholson, M. (2015) 'Cicada 3301: CIA Recruitment Tool or the Internet's Greatest Practical Joke?' [online] *Second Nexus.* Available at: https://secondnexus.com/science/cicada-3301-cia-recruitment-game-internets-greatest-practical-joke [Accessed 24 February 2020]

Osenlund, R.K. (2019) '*The OA* May Have Been Cancelled but Few Shows Can Claim the Same Social Impact' [online] *Observer.* Available at: https://observer.com/2019/08/the-oa-netflix-canceled-brit-marling-message-petition-movement/ [Accessed 27 May 2020]

Pirandello, L. (1995) *Six Characters in Search of an Author and Other Plays.* London: Penguin Books.

Power, E. (2019) '*The OA*, season 2 review: Netflix's weird inter-dimensional soap opera is now even weirder' [online] *Telegraph.* Available at https://www.telegraph.co.uk/on-demand/0/oa-season-2-review-netflixs-weirdinter-dimensional-soap-opera/ [Accessed 3 February 2020]

Renfro, K. (2019) '*The OA* star Ian Alexander helps explain Buck's confounding final scene: "It's very meta"' [online] *Insider.* Available at https://www.insider.com/the-oa-buck-ian-alexander-interview-netflix-2019-3 [Accessed 27 May 2020]

Robinson, J. (1996) *The Nag Hammadi Library in English.* Leiden; New York; Köln: E.J. Brill.

Sadler, S. (1999) *The Situationist City.* Cambridge, MA: The MIT Press.

Saraiya, S. (2016) TV Review: Netflix's *The OA* [online] *Variety.* Available at https://variety.com/2016/tv/reviews/tv-review-netflix-the-oa-brit-marling-1201941411/ [Accessed 2 May 2020]

Sauve, M. (2016) *Who Authored the John Titor Legend? An Investigation Into the John Titor Time Travel Posts*. Big Swerve Press.

Schwartz J. & Thomsen, Brian M. (2000) *Man of Two Worlds: My Life in Science Fiction and Comics*. New York: HarperCollins.

Seale, J. (2019) 'The OA season two review – the psychic octopus is the final straw' [online] *Guardian*. Available at https://www.theguardian.com/tv-and-radio/2019/mar/22/the-oa-season-two-review-netflix-brit-marling [Accessed 24 April 2020]

Sense8 (2015-2018) [TV series] Created by The Wachowskis; J. Michael Straczynski. US: Netflix.

Shaviro, S. (2005) 'Once More with Feeling' [online] *The Pinocchio Theory*. Available at http://www.shaviro.com/Blog/?p=406 [Accessed 27 March 2020]

-(2010) *Post Cinematic Affect*. Winchester, UK: Zero Books.

-(2011) Hyperbolic Futures: Speculative Finance and Speculative Fiction [online] *The Cascadia Subduction Zone*. Available at https://thecsz.com/past-issues/csz-v1-n2-2011.pdf [Accessed 23 March 2020]

Sliders (1995-2000) [TV series] Created by Robert K. Weiss; Tracy Tormé. US: Fox; Sci-Fi Channel.

Spring (2014) [film] Directed by Justin Benson; Aaron Moorhead. US: Drafthouse Films.

St. Elsewhere (1982-1988) [TV series] Created by Joshua Brand, John Falsey. US: MTM Enterprises.

Steele, E.J.; Al-Mufti, S.; Augustyn, K.A. et al (2018) 'Cause of Cambrian Explosion: Terrestrial or Cosmic?' [online] *Progress in Biophysics and Molecular Biology*. Available at https://www.sciencedirect.com/science/article/pii/S0079610718300798?via%3Dihub [Accessed 13 February 2020]

Stevenson, R.L. (1886) *The Strange Case of Dr Jekyll and Mr Hyde*. London: Longmans, Green & Co.

Stranger Things (2016-) [TV series] Created by The Duffer Brothers. US: Netflix.

Sweeney, D. (2015) '"Your face looks backwards": Time Travel Cinema, Nostalgia and the End of History' [online] *Thesis 11*. Available at https://journals.sagepub.com/doi/abs/10.1177/0725513615613456 [Accessed 24 February 2020]

Symonds, A. (2016) 'Character Building: Brit Marling' [online] *The New York Times Style Magazine*. Available at: https://www.nytimes.com/2016/12/16/t-magazine/entertainment/the-oa-brit-marling-netflix.html [Accessed 24 March 2020]

Tate, K. (2015) 'How Lewis Carroll's "Syzygy" Puzzles Worked' [online] *Live Science*. Available at: https://www.livescience.com/51437-how-lewis-carroll-s-syzygy-puzzles-worked-infographic.html [Accessed 14 February 2020]

Taylor. G. (2019) 'Review: *The OA* Part 2' [online] The Daily Grail. Available at https://www.dailygrail.com/2019/03/review-the-oa-part-2/ [Accessed 29 March 2020]

Travers, B. (2018) 'The OA Season 2: Netflix VP Says "Fans Will Be Very Happy" with New Episodes and Confirms Five-Season Plan' [online] Indiewire. Available at https://www.indiewire.com/2018/07/the-oa-season-2-netflix-fantastic-five-season-plan-1201989088/ [Accessed 14 February 2020].

True Detective (2017-2019) [TV series] created by Nic Pizzolatto. US: HBO.

The Twilight Zone (1959-1964) [TV series] Created by Rod Serling. US: CBS.

-(2019) [TV series] Developed by Simon Kinberg; Jordan Peele; Marco Ramirez. US: CBS All Access.

Twin Peaks (1990-1991) [TV series] Created by Mark Frost; David Lynch. US: ABC.

Twin Peaks: The Return (2017) [TV series] Created by Mark Frost; David Lynch. US: Showtime.

Viscardi, J. (2018) 'Mark Millar talks Millarworld, Netflix and What Happens Next' [online] Comicbook.com. Available at https://comicbook.com/movies/news/mark-millar-talks-millarworld-netflix-and-what-happens-next/ [Accessed 24 February 2020]

Weber, W. (2003) General Economic Theory: The Social Causes of the Decay of Ancient Civilisation. Mineola, NY: Dover Publications Inc., [1927].

-(2012 [1947]) The Theory of Social and Economic Organization. New York, NY: The Free Press.

Zuboff, S. (2019) Surveillance Capitalism: The Fight for a Human Future at the New Frontier of Power. London: Profile Books.

zulawski (2020) The OA Part III [online] Available at: https://archiveofourown.org/works/22434136/chapters/53601733 [Accessed 26 May 2020].